T0137496

CHOOSE

LIFE TO THE FULLEST

*90 DAYS TO THINKING
AND LIVING GREAT*

BECCA GUNYON, MCC

WESTBOW
PRESS®
A DIVISION OF THOMAS NELSON
& ZONDERVAN

WestBow Press books may be ordered through booksellers or by contacting:

WestBow Press
A Division of Thomas Nelson & Zondervan
1663 Liberty Drive
Bloomington, IN 47403
www.westbowpress.com
1 (866) 928-1240

ISBN: 978-1-9736-7913-4 (sc)
ISBN: 978-1-9736-7914-1 (e)

Print information available on the last page.

WestBow Press rev. date: 11/12/2019

PURPOSE

"The secret conversations you hold in the privacy of your own mind are shaping your destiny, little by little. With every thought that races through your mind, you are continually reinventing yourself and your future. Research indicates that the average person thinks approximately fifty thousand thoughts per day. This is either good or bad news because every thought moves you either toward your God-given potential or away from it. No thoughts are neutral."

— Tommy Newberry (The 4:8 Principle)

"We can change the physical nature of our brain through our thinking and choosing." Dr. Caroline Leaf (Switch On Your Brain)

Choosing life to the fullest is about waking up and thinking great, inviting Jesus into our day, and finding ourselves in His identity. Amazing repetitive thoughts are key to this process.

My passion in writing this compilation started with thinking about my own teenage thoughts and how they affected my journey. Which led me to ask myself, would my own teenagers and students that I mentor read a daily, short, thought-changing devotion?

What is the purpose of Choose Life to the Fullest?

After studying authors much wiser than myself, I found that when we wake up and think five great thoughts our brain starts changing. These five great thoughts super-charge our brain. The opposite is true when we wake up and think five defeating thoughts, we start the day behind.

We are not victim to our thoughts, we get to choose them. As Christians, when we invite Jesus into this process, life-change happens.

"For as he thinks within himself, so he is." (Proverbs 23:7 NASB)

Dedicated to my husband Dan, who wakes up every morning and writes ten things he is thankful for

Thank yous:

Thankful to Lexie Fish for editing each devotion
Thankful to Madison Smith and Owin Gunyon for editing sections
Thankful to Addi Gunyon for designing all the Instagram posts @ chooselifetothefullest
Thankful to Westbow Publishing for being so wonderful to work with
Thankful to Travis Fish for designing the cover
Thankful to my husband, Dan, who encourages me to write daily
Thankful for my son, Owin, who edits my books and encourages me to live my dreams
Thankful for my daughter, Addi, who creates beauty and speaks Jesus back to me
Thankful to my son, Eben, who thanks me daily for being me
Thankful to my son, John E, who flatters me with his funny compliments
Thankful to my son, Anden, who asks me if I have thought good thoughts today
Thankful to all the teenagers that previewed and gave their opinion
Thankful to my family, our circle of closeness is a blessing- (Jim and Danise Owings, Josh and Meredith Owings, Matt and Abi Tuiasosopo, Micah Owings, JonMark Owings and all my sweet nephews)

ENDORSEMENTS

"There is nothing worth fighting for more than the faith of the next generation. After spending years in student ministry, I came to the conclusion that there has never been a more challenging time to grow up than now. Countless things compete daily for our attention and slowly cause us to drift from the things that matter most. I have known Becca and her family for decades and have always respected their commitment to the next generation. Paul told us that we can be transformed by the renewal of our minds. I believe this book help us to see what is looks like to practically tap into the power that Paul was talking about. This is a great resource that will strengthen your entire family." - *Grant Patrick, Passion City Church, Location Pastor // Cumberland*

"As we coach and care for the teenagers in our lives, not much is more important than encouraging them to practice renewing their minds. Becca's focus on spending a few moments each day to reflect on God's truth and focus on gratitude is a life changing practice not only for the young people who will build this habit, but also for the parents who're praying them through these tough years. I'm so excited for her to share these insights with a generation of kids who are hungry for them! - *Natalie Kitchen (North Point Leadership Experience- Residency Program Director and mother of three)*

"It's not often you get to walk through life watching a person live out the passion they had in them even as a young child. I've had that unique opportunity with my older sister Becca. She was nearly four years old when I was born, and instead of jealousy toward me, she loved me from the day I came home. Our friendship grew stronger as we got older, and she was always a safe place for me to share my heart, reminding me that God loves me and pursues me regardless of the choices or mistakes I make. Becca helped me learn to see myself through God's eyes and not other's or my own. Her gentle kindness and servant spirit for God shine through her daily as she pours her life and heart into others more than herself. This book is Gods heart through her pen, expressing the aspiration she has for all people, that they journey to a daily relationship with God, learning to love themselves the way God loves them, and in turn live their life to the fullest." - *Josh Owings, CEO/Owings Enterprises LLC*

"After working in middle school ministry for a number of years, you start to realize there could never be enough resources to help remind students that they have an opportunity to choose their thoughts and think, "great!" Becca invites you to choose Life to the Fullest by waking up and thinking great thoughts again, and again. I could not recommend this book highly enough!" - *Lexie Fish (Worship Leader and Project Manager of Gwinnett Church Transit)*

"As a parent, I believe it is life changing and something I will have to instill in my life and my children's lives. The concept of Living Life to the Fullest is a continuous process, that we need to be reminded of often. As a teacher, I Love this book and the message it is trying to get across to students. Too many people do not know how to live/experience life to the fullest. It is a lifelong process and skill! Without God, we are nothing!!!!!!!!!!!!!!!!!!!" - *Dr. Natalie Gibson (teacher, mother, leader in student ministry)*

"I love that these devotionals start off reminding us to look for things to be thankful for, and then they examine a truth from Scripture & give students a practical way to apply it to their own lives. This will be a blessing to all who read it!" - *Janet Payton (mother of three teenagers)*

"God's heart for us all shines so beautifully through the words found in each devotional. Becca has humbly submitted her spirit, soul and body to declaring Gods truths in a simple, concise and easy to understand manner. The words cut through the chaos and distractions of life to refocus our minds, souls and spirits according to our true identity in Christ. Each devotional redirects our minds away from the lies of the enemy and this world back towards the truth which can only come from right believing and a personal relationship with Jesus. I'm blessed to be ministered to by such a courageous, faithful servant of God." - *Zenda Griebenow, (Director and Tennis Coach- Zen Tennis)*

Words from Students (their words, their age, and something they enjoy)-

"Choose Life to the Fullest has changed the way I think throughout the day. Every time I start to get down or think negative thoughts I remember to change them and focus on what's good. I have been 100% happier and I enjoy life more after reading and applying this book." - *Owin/age 17/Baseball*

"Having struggled through difficult feelings such as heartbreak, depression, and anxiety myself, this book reminded me that God has given us the ability to *choose* an abundant life, despite the hardships we face. I was reminded that feelings are not always truth, and feelings do *not* control us! Through reading this, I was encouraged to stand up to lies in practical ways." - *Madison/College Student*

"These daily devotions have impacted me emotionally and mentally. Whenever I feel like nothing can go my way. I think of the phrases and topics of the devotions and God always helps me power through it. All it takes is 5 minutes every day and I feel like a stronger person after." - *Derek/age 16/baseball*

"The 5 questions are the beginning of the devos help me to focus. Sometimes when I read the Bible, my mind will wander, but this not the case with Choose Life to the Fullest. It helps me to actively align myself with what God will teach me that day. I face a lot at school and this may be the only positive word I receive all day." - *JP/ age 16/ baseball and crossfit*

"I like them because they are short, powerful, and straight to the point. I get distracted and sleepy if people go on and on." - *Toler/ age 13/crossfit and cross country*

"This devotional book is really making me think about Choosing Joy." - *August /age 11/reading Harry Potter*

"I never thought about a lot of these questions." - *Pierce/age 10/ baseball*

"This is a fantastic devotional. I love the interaction for the daily question (What are 3 or 5 things?) It really made me think. It really helped me focus on casting aside fears and focusing on God?" - *Emily/age13/loves riding horses*

"This devotional starts my day off with positivity and the right attitude. It reminds me daily of God's love for me and the people He has blessed me with." - *Ivan/age 16/basketball*

"Mom, I woke up this morning and started thinking of 5 things I was thankful for." - *Eben/age 13/tennis*

"Life to the fullest has not just made an impact on the way I view myself, it has made a pivotal turn in my relationships with others. We can often start our day off on the wrong foot, but these daily devotionals have made a positive start to every day." - *Savannah/ age 18/spending time outdoors*

"I believe that our thoughts effect the way we live our life. Sometimes it's difficult to change our negative thoughts and think positive. Choose life to the fullest is very encouraging and includes amazing advice for changing your thoughts." - *Addi Gunyon/15/loves basketball, tennis, art*

Choosing great thoughts
+ Inviting Jesus in=

LIFE TO THE FULLEST

DAY 1

What are 5 things I enjoy? (take a second to write your answers)

1.
2.
3.
4.
5.

Jesus said, "I came so they can have real and eternal life, more and better life than they ever dreamed of." (John 10:10 MSG)

What did He mean by this? What would make your life better?

Our life gets better as we think better. This combination, of repeatedly *thinking about great things* and *inviting Jesus into* our lives, is life-changing. It changes the way that we treat others, the way that we think about ourselves, the way we perform in sports and hobbies, how well we do in school, and our quality of life. We can choose to start everyday with FIVE great thoughts, this jump-starts our brains and helps us feel good about the day.

After thinking about great things in our life, we can take a moment to connect with God by inviting Him into our day. "To advance in life, first retreat with God." (Tommy Newberry)

A simple prayer:

Jesus, I invite You into my life to start showing me what this means "real life, better than I ever dreamed of." In Jesus name

What are 5 good things in my life?

1.
2.
3.
4.
5.

"Jesus said, 'Come and see.'" (John 1:39 WE)

Jesus gave an invitation to "come and see." He extends the same invitation to us.

Life can taint our view of God. We might not totally understand Jesus, which is okay, neither did the disciples. Yet when Jesus was here on earth, He always had a crowd following Him. Everyone wanted to be with Him. Something about Him was so remarkable people left everything to hang out with Him. Spending time getting to know Jesus is life-changing.

Will I accept His invitation to "come and see?" If not, why?

What do I think about God that makes me keep Him at a distance?

Where did my view of God come from?

God, show up in my life. Show me more of who You are. I accept Your invitation and I invite You to show me Jesus.

(For additional reading: John 1; recommended version The Message Bible)

DAY 3

What in my life is good?

1.
2.
3.
4.
5.

"The thief comes only to steal and kill and destroy; I (Jesus) have come that they may have life, and have it to the full." (John 10:10 NIV)

Life "to the full" is what God offers. The thief is the enemy (his constant negative voice, his temptation...)

★God wants us to have a great life. God is not to blame when life is hard. He told us life would be hard, but He would walk through it with us.

"Life to the full" begins with realizing that God is good, Jesus wants to be in relationship with us, and we don't need to be a victim of the negative thoughts and temptations that come our way.

You get to choose your thoughts about everything!

Thinking great about life, yourself, future, your friends, and God changes everything in amazing ways. Today let's REPEATEDLY think about: "what's good in my life?"

God, show me You are good. Change any negative thoughts that I have about You. In Jesus name

DAY 4

What are 3 things in my life that make me smile?

1.
2.
3.

(Take a moment to think about each of these things.)

"Never will I leave you…" (Hebrews 13:5 NIV)

On the good days and the bad days, God is with us. Somewhere along the way this became what I first think of when I wake up. I hear a tender but strong whisper, "I am here." This thought makes me feel like Someone is with me to walk through whatever life throws my way.

Life is full of the unexpected, yet we have the God of all to walk through it with us. God did not abandon us to figure life out alone. He wants to walk through the moments (good and bad) with us.

It is our choice to invite Him into our lives, in our thoughts, our hopes, our school and workplace, our relationships, our discouragements, our dreams, our failures, our struggles...

What is a struggle that you can invite God into today?

God, You are with me. Sometimes, I forget that I am not alone. In the morning, start my day off by thinking You are good, You are for me, and You will help me. In Jesus name

Who makes me smile?

Why? (Thinking about great relationships makes us thankful.)

"God is love." (1 John 4:8 NIV)

If God had DNA, it would be love. He is full of love for us. Life is not always good, people hurt us. This is not a reflection of God. **God has complete unconditional, passionate, pursuing, tender, powerful love for us.** He made us, He loves us. When we let His love heal the pain that life brings, everything changes.

What painful thing do you repeatedly think about?

Replaying painful events or words in our mind is something that we don't even realize that we do, yet it steals our joy. Our thoughts about hurtful situations can keep us feeling sad. We can choose to give each painful memory or situation to Him. Asking His love to heal our deepest wound is so powerful. Every time we remember, we can give it to Him again, and think about the good in our life.

What painful event or memory can I give to God?

Life is hard, still God's love rescues us from every pain!

God, I give You my painful memory. I don't want to replay it in my mind anymore. When I am replaying hurtful memories, remind me to think about the great things in my life. May Your love fill my heart, healing the pain. In Jesus name

What do I love? (three things- take 10 seconds to think about these things)

1.
2.
3.

"And so we know and rely on the love God has for us." (1 John 4:16 NIV)

"If we really understand the magnitude of God's love, we are naturally drawn to Him. We want to be with Him. Following Him is our instinct response. We desire to sit with Him and take Him everywhere we go. If we view God as a safe Protector and tender lover of our souls. He draws us in. If we imagine His friendly countenance, we want to hang out with Him. If we see God as He really is portrayed in the life of Jesus lived here, then God is tender, strong, caring, powerful, compassionate, aware of our needs, and relational. God is love!" (The Treasure)

Our view of God effects everything. If we see God as Someone who is good and for us, we see life as good. If we wrap our minds in His love and care for us, we like ourselves. Accepting His love and letting it become our identity is life-changing. His love is a strong foundation for our self-worth.

What is my view of God?

What gave me this view of Him?

Do I think my picture of God is accurate?

God, show me more of who You really are. Life's disappointments and unkind people have skewed my view of You. I invite You to show me who You are and help this to change how I see me. In Jesus name

What are 5 great things in my life?

1.
2.
3.
4.
5.

"...He (Jesus) displayed His greatness and His power openly and His disciples believed in Him (adhered to, trusted in, and relied on Him)." (John 2:11 AMPC)

What do I trust, rely on, stick to?

Does this help me?

In every area of my life, what would it look like to stick to, trust in, and rely on God today?

What would this change?

I find that when I trust in me, I fall short in so many ways. Yet, it is life-changing to stick to God and rely on Him. His motivation, His love, His grace, His goodness, His patience, His truths...

If we think about all the ways where we are "not enough" we can live defeated.

In what area do you feel like you are "not enough" in your life?

In contrast, our life is empowered when we whisper throughout the day to God asking Him to help us where we just don't feel _____ (whatever thing that challenges us). This practice changes our thinking in amazing ways!

Jesus, I trust in YOU! I want to desire to rely on You instead of myself. I invite You into my heart, my life, my thoughts, and my day. Please show me the heart of God. In Jesus name

What is best in my life?

1.
2.
3.
4.
5.

"filling your minds and meditating on things true, noble, reputable, authentic, compelling, gracious—the best, not the worst;" (Phil. 4:8 MSG)

"The best not the worst" needs to be our focus. We can choose what we focus on, we can choose what we think about, we can have life "to the full" if we choose it.

What do you currently choose to think about your life and your future? Do these thoughts make your life feel better?

What we repeatedly think about (life, God, ourselves) either gives us "life to the full" or an empty life - always searching.

What would it look like to think "the best" about ourselves, our family, our siblings, our parents, our sport or hobby, our school/workplace, our church, our friends, our God?

We can focus on "the BEST!"

God, please enter my thoughts and help me to think the best thoughts. Give me "life to the full." Show me Your grace and love. In Jesus name

What are 5 things that I am thankful for?

1.
2.
3.
4.
5.

"Don't be afraid, just believe." (Jesus spoke this. Mark 5:36 NIV)

When I was sixteen years old, I was given a new Bible, it had my name engraved on the front, it was a beautiful gift. Yet, it was overwhelming. Where do I start reading? It's so thick! How do these verses or stories apply to my life?

It sat by my bed for six months and then one day I opened it. A wise friend told me to take one verse and sit in it.

For instance: the verse above, "don't be afraid, just believe."

We can ask ourselves:

What does this mean for me?

What am I afraid of?

What does "just believe" Jesus look like for me?

What about Jesus makes me know I can trust Him?

We can connect with God by sitting in one small verse, inviting Jesus in, and thinking He is good. Somewhere along the way- this practice changes us in amazing ways!

God, thank You that when I read about You I see who You are. I invite You to remind me of You throughout the day. In Jesus name

DAY 10

What makes me happy?

1.
2.
3.
4.
5.

"Who makes everything complete, Who fills everything everywhere with Himself." (Eph. 1:23 AMPC)

This verse is talking about Jesus, I had to read it twice. He "fills."

So many of us look for false fillers: achievement, approval, food, social media, success, addiction…

If there is an emptiness inside of us, it's because the love of Jesus is yet to fill that canyon in our souls. If you know about God or grew up in church you might have given your life to Jesus by saying, "I believe in You (Your death on the cross and resurrection), please forgive me for my sins, and I give You me." At that moment, we become Christians.

However, the Christian life is a journey. Some of us have God inside of us, but have forgotten about that prayer of surrender. Or maybe our negative thoughts seem louder than God.

Do I ever feel empty?

Jesus, continually fills us with His love, His hope, and His joy. It is our choice to dive into His love, choose our thoughts, and invite Him in to fill everything in our life.

God, I want to dive into Your love, choose Your thoughts, and invite You in to "fill everything" in my life. In Jesus name

DAY 11

What makes me smile and why?

1.

2.

3.

"...Don't feel bad. The joy of GOD *is your strength!" (Neh. 8:10 MSG)*

You get to choose how you feel. Your thoughts will determine your feelings. If you think about the great things in your life your feelings will follow. How do you feel today?

What am I thinking about?

Can I see how my thoughts and feelings are connected?

If I think about the bad things in my life my feelings will follow. I get to CHOOSE!!!

What do I think about most of the time? What feeling does this lead to?

Thinking about the good around us leads to feeling good about life. We can always find the good, even if we have to search for it.

God, I want to feel good. I ask You to invade my thought life. I want to choose great thoughts. Remind me throughout the day, that You are good and You are for me. In Jesus name

What are 5 AMAZING things in my life?

1.
2.
3.
4.
5.

*"Do not conform to the pattern of this world, but be transformed by the **renewing** of your **mind**. Then you will be able to test and approve what God's will is—his good, pleasing and perfect will." (Romans 12:2 NIV)*

This is a secret to an amazing life. It is so simple, yet it changes everything!

First: *Ask yourself: What negative thought do I replay about myself?* I am guessing this thought effects everything you do, it did for me.

Second: *When that negative thought starts in your brain say, "STOP!"* The thought stops.

Third: *think a great "go to" thought about you.*

For example: I am a child of God, God has great things planned for me, I am a champion, I am a treasure, I am loved. Or find a song with great lyrics.

At age 19, I started doing this, my "go to" thought was, "define myself radically as one beloved by God, His love defines my worth" (paraphrased quote in *Abba's Child* by Brennan Manning). I must have told myself that phrase thousands of times to combat the negative thoughts I constantly battled.

Fourth: *Repeat steps 1-3 over and over again.*

These steps will change your life FOREVER!

God, help me to take my thoughts back by thinking great things about life, You, and me. In Jesus name

5 things I am thankful for are:

1.
2.
3.
4.
5.

And He arose and rebuked the wind and said to the sea, Hush now! Be still (muzzled)! And the wind ceased (sank to rest as if exhausted by its beating) and there was [immediately] a great calm (a perfect peacefulness). He said to them, Why are you so timid and fearful? How is it that you have no faith (no firmly relying trust)?" (Mark 4:39-40 AMPC)

Jesus must have had a strong voice. Using only His voice and words, He spoke to stop the storm. Yet I believe His strong voice was tender. I wonder if it bothered Jesus that His friends did not trust Him. He cared that they were afraid. He cared how they reacted to the storm.

What is the storm in my life?

How am I reacting?

God cares. Can I trust God to ask Him for help?

God, please calm the storm in my life. I believe that You can do miracles. In Jesus name

What are 5 things I enjoy?

1.
2.
3.
4.
5.

When I read the stories of when Jesus walked here on Earth, often I wonder: what did His voice sound like. What about Him drew a huge crowd? When He looked at people did they feel truly loved and treasured in such a way that made them want to follow Him for days?

We can take stories (from the Bible) and ask ourselves questions. In doing this, we see more of Jesus.

For instance: when Jesus said, *"Therefore I tell you, do not worry about your life..." (Matthew 6:25 NIV)* He knew people were worried about their life and all the "stuff" that goes with it.

What did His voice sound like when He told them not to worry?

What do I worry about?

Do I think of His voice as being gentle with me even if I am struggling? Why or Why not?

God cares, He wants to give us His peace in exchange for our worry, anxiety and fears.

God in His compassion sent Jesus to show us a loving God who would care about our stuff.

Jesus, please show me more of who You are. I give You _____ (what I worry about). In Jesus name

(Suggested Reading about Jesus: the book of John in the New Testament)

What am I thankful for?

1.
2.
3.
4.
5.

"This, the first of His signs (miracles, wonderworks), Jesus performed in Cana of Galilee, and manifested His glory (by it He displayed His greatness and His power openly), and His disciples believed in Him (adhered to, trusted in, and relied on Him.)" (John 2:11 AMPC)

The first miracle Jesus performed was at a party. His mom asked Him to provide more drinks. This amazes me: His first miracle was about helping people enjoy life!

Let's think about this:

Why did God choose this to be the first miracle?

Could it have been because God wanted to show us something about Himself?

Maybe His first miracle was about meeting a need that may seem small, but was important to people. Maybe it was just because His mom asked Him to. I am not sure of the reason, but I am amazed that Jesus cared enough to meet a small need. God doesn't just want our big stuff, He wants us to give Him our small needs.

What do I need God to do in my life?

What small needs swirl in my mind?

Do I think God cares about everything - or just the big stuff? Why?

Jesus showed His greatness in this story, which led to His disciples (friends) making a choice. They "relied on Him."

God, I know You care about the small things in my life. I need You to do something big in this situation. I want to rely on You and think great about You- take away my doubts and any negative thoughts that I have about You, I want to know Your heart. In Jesus name

DAY 16

What are 5 gifts in my life?

1.
2.
3.
4.
5.

"Every desirable and beneficial gift comes out of heaven. The gifts are rivers of light cascading down from the Father of Light. There is nothing deceitful in God, nothing two-faced, nothing fickle. He brought us to life using the true Word, showing us off as the crown of all his creatures."
(James 1:17-18 MSG)

God was "showing off" when He made you. Regardless of how you feel, the truth is you are a gift. If we remember God gave us every gift, we will see Him as good. If we focus on our gifts instead of what we don't have– our perspective changes. Then we can be a gift to others.

Do I focus on what I have or what I don't have?

How does this affect me?

God, thank You for every good gift, help me to remember that I am a gift to You and others. In Jesus name

What are 5 qualities that I possess?

1.
2.
3.
4.
5.

"But the fruit of the Spirit [the result of His presence within us] is love [unselfish concern for others], joy, [inner] peace, patience [not the ability to wait, but how we act while waiting], kindness, goodness, faithfulness, gentleness, self-control." (Gal. 5:22-23 AMP)

When we invite God's presence in our lives His qualities become part of us. We start changing on the inside, which shows up in the way we treat others. When we know and believe we are loved by the tender powerful Creator of the Universe, His love SPILLS out of us.

Do I possess these fruits/qualities? In what ways?

Which one is the most difficult for me?

God, I want Your qualities. Please give me your love, joy, peace, patience, kindness, goodness, faithfulness, gentleness, self-control. In Jesus name

What are 3 things that are good in my life- that I enjoy daily?

1.
2.
3.

"Be cheerful no matter what." (1 Thes. 5:16 MSG)

This verse involves a choice. We get to choose our mood. We do not have to let our mood control us. If we wake up sad or anxious, we can choose to focus on the great things in our life, invite God in, and repeat the process. It is not easy, but repeatedly choosing to think about the good drives out the sad, depressing, dead-end thoughts.

What is my mood the majority of the time?

Does this reflect my thoughts?

God, thank you that I get to choose my thoughts. Help me to share laughter wherever I go. I bet Jesus laughed a lot when He was here on earth and everyone wanted to be with Him, please make me someone that people want to be with because I am filled with Your happiness. In Jesus name

Who in my life encourages me?

1.
2.
3.

"For as he thinks within himself, so he is." (Proverbs 23:7 NASB)

We live out our thoughts. If we think happy, we live with happiness. If we think angry, we live frustrated. If we think hateful thoughts, they come out. If we think badly of ourselves, it effects our posture, our actions, and whether we are kind to others. If we think about the bad instead of the great our life will seem miserable.

We get to choose what we think!

If our thoughts are stuck in yuck, we can change them one at a time. If we think, "I hate this person." We can immediately STOP and instead think this person must be hurting, their hurt does not need to effect and wound me.

How can I be kind, instead of returning hate? Repeatedly STOPPING and CHANGING our thoughts about others will give us a great life.

Who in my life is challenging?

What are they going through that might be effecting the way that they treat me?

God, I invite You in to my thoughts to stop the bad thoughts and remind me of the good and great things. In Jesus name

*Refocusing what we think throughout the day is life-giving. When a negative thought pops in our mind we can choose to let is stay there or to refocus. This repetitive practice will give us an amazing life.

What are 5 things that I love?

1.
2.
3.
4.
5.

"God is love." (1 John 4:8 ESV)

Who is someone that truly loves me? God is not a human, He is perfect. He has perfect love, grace, and truth for us. When we stop blaming Him for the bad stuff in life and start asking Him to bring healing and help, something in us changes.

Our perception of God changes everything. If we believe God is for us, our view of every single aspect of life changes.

Do I feel like God has let me down?

Do I blame Him for the way people have treated me or my pain?

Can I choose to think "God is for me!"?

God, change the way I see You. I am sorry for blaming You for life's pain. I know that You are complete Love. Help me to see You this way when life does not feel good. In Jesus name

What 7 things am I thankful for?

1.
2.
3.
4.
5.
6.
7.

"If God is for us, who can be against us?" (Romans 8:31 NIV)

At times, it can feel like everyone is against us and life is falling apart. However, God is always for us, working to pursue us, and wants to walk beside us. We can either blame God for life being hard or invite Him to fix the hard. He warns us that because of sin and darkness this world will be hard, yet He promises to always be with us. God is for us- today, tomorrow, to heal our yesterday.

What would change in my life if I believed God is for me?

God, show me that You are for me. Fill my heart with Jesus. In His name

Who are 5 people that I am thankful for?

1.
2.
3.
4.
5.

"Thank God no matter what happens. This is the way God wants you who belong to Christ Jesus to live." (1 Thess. 5:17-18 MSG)

Whether we feel like life is what we want it to be like or not—we can find things to be thankful for. (We have enough food, a warm bed, a person who loves us...)

Choosing thankfulness changes our thoughts, which changes our believe system, which changes our behavior, and THIS changes our life! All counselors learn this in school. If you get this concept, you could be a counselor. ☺

If our thoughts are great – we will have a GREAT life!

Who in my life is always thankful?

Do I like being around them?

God, Thank you for_____ In Jesus name

What are 5 great things about me?

1.
2.
3.
4.
5.

*"For we are God's **masterpiece**. He has created us anew in Christ Jesus, so we can do the good things he planned for us long ago." (Ephesians 2:10 NLT)*

A few words that describe a masterpiece are: "a prize, a gem, a wonder, a work of art." God sees us as His masterpiece. God does not see all the flaws we see, He sees a work of art. When we start seeing ourselves through His eyes-we start seeing ourselves differently. We are not a mistake, we are not flawed, we are not messed up, we are not a disappointment. We are created by the Creator who made waterfalls and fireflies. You are magnificent!

What would change if I thought of myself as a masterpiece? As magnificent?

God, I want to see myself through Your eyes. Remind me that You made me unique, talented, incredible and stop me when I start to dwell on the things I don't like about me. In Jesus name

What are 10 things that are good in my life?

_____

_____

_____

_____

Let's think about this verse again today.

"For we are God's **masterpiece**. He has created us anew in Christ Jesus, so we can do the good things he planned for us long ago." (Ephesians 2:10 NLT)

Okay, so if we are a masterpiece we can believe that God has great things planned for us. Whether life looks like it is going well or not, we can believe God has a great future for us. Belief involves a choice, not a feeling. We can either stress about all of the things ahead of us or we can CHOOSE to trust God.

Easier said than done, right? Do I believe God's heart for me is good?

Do I believe He has great plans for me?

If we are a "masterpiece," why wouldn't God have greatness for us?

Following God has no dead-end roads. Following God is an adventure and at times is full of unknowns, so even amidst the unknown, we must trust His heart for us is good.

God, what did you "plan for me long ago?" What do you have for me? Help me to trust Your heart as you show me Your plan. In Jesus name

What am I thankful for?

1.
2.
3.
4.
5.

"...*He has created us anew in Christ Jesus, so we can do the good things he planned for us long ago.*" *(Ephesians 2:10 NLT) (again same verse as yesterday)*

He planned good things for us!

The second greatest commandment states, "Love one another." (John 13:34 NIV)

What does this mean?

We can start with taking the focus off- of ourselves and find someone to do "good" to. We can pick a family member, a friend, someone who seems down, anyone.

This probably sounds silly, but my phone reminds me every few hours to "be the blessing." This phrase reminds me, to quit focusing on my own stuff and go bless someone. These three words "be the blessing" interrupt my selfish thoughts, my worry, my insecurity. This reminder puts a smile on my face and leads to this question:

What can I say or do right now that would bless someone?
(Who can you bless right now?)

What phrase could you put on your phone as a reminder to "do good" to others?

Blessing, helping, thanking, reaching out - does something mysterious to our own souls. When we are doing good to others-we feel better, because we think better, which leads to living BETTER!

May we challenge ourselves to pick one person a day to do something good for.

God, remind me to look outside of my stuff to do good to others, I invite You to interrupt my selfish thoughts. In Jesus name

What are three things that bless me?

1.
2.
3.

"This resurrection life you received from God is not a timid, grave-tending life. It's adventurously expectant, greeting God with a childlike "What's next, Papa?" God's Spirit touches our spirits and confirms who we really are. We know who he is, and we know who we are: Father and children. And we know we are going to get what's coming to us—an unbelievable inheritance!" (Romans 8:15-17 MSG)

I love adventure! Don't you? God has an adventure for us. He wants us to ask Him, "What's next?" He is the good Father, the perfect Father, the loving Father. HE has goodness in store for His kids. He knows our heart better than we do, so He knows what will make our heart happy, joyful and fulfilled!

Have I ever thought of God being adventurous?

Can you trust God to say, "Okay, I choose what You have for me. I choose faith and trusting You with me." (If this is hard to say to God- why?)

God, I give You me. I want Your adventure. I want to have a full heart. In Jesus name

Who can I bless, help, thank, reach out to today?

What can I celebrate today?

_____

"Celebrate God all day, every day. I mean, revel in him! Make it as clear as you can to all you meet that you're on their side, working with them and not against them. Help them see that the Master is about to arrive. He could show up any minute." (Phil. 4:8-9 MSG)

Celebrating is something we forget to do. Celebrating progress is huge in keeping us going. If we only focus on where we are not, we will get discouraged. But if we focus on each step of progress, we will be motivated to keep going.

What progress have I made lately?

Today, in the area that I am striving in –how can I celebrate the journey?

By living our lives with joy and passion, we will celebrate God. As we strive toward our goals and dreams, may we know that true life and worth is found in knowing that God loves us and He has great things for us.

God, I want to celebrate. Help me to celebrate the life that You have given me. in Jesus name

Who can I bless, help, thank, reach out to today?

What are 5 great things I see every day?

1.
2.
3.
4.
5.

"…Make it as clear as you can to all you meet that you're on their side, working with them and not against them. Help them see that the Master is about to arrive. He could show up any minute." (Phil. 4:8-9 MSG)

We live around and with people – some are easy to live with; others, not so much.

Looking past someone's actions and words to their heart is a powerful tool to change our perspective. We grow in compassion for people who annoy us when we look at their story, their life, their failure, their pain. Repeatedly looking at others' hearts changes the way we think about them. Compassion grows!

Who can I think differently about today? What is their pain?

How can we show people we are "on their side?" How can we think the best of others around us whether we like feel it or not?

God, I invite You into the way I see _____. Sometimes they really annoy me. Please give me compassion, please heal their pain. In Jesus name

Who can I bless, help, thank, reach out to today?

What 5 things do I treasure?

1.
2.
3.
4.
5.

"However, you are chosen people, a royal priesthood, a holy nation, people who belong to God. You were chosen to tell about the excellent qualities of God, who called you out of darkness into his marvelous light." (1 Peter 2:9 GW)

Do I see myself as chosen? Do I feel like I have a purpose?

We become a Christian by believing in Jesus and saying a prayer such as, "I give all I know of me to all I know of You. Please forgive my sins. I believe You died on the cross and were resurrected."

After saying this prayer or a similar prayer, we become part of God's family, WE "belong to God."

God has an amazing purpose for each of us. Here He calls His kids (us) "royal." We were chosen for something that He has planned for us. His plans are always magnificent!

God, help me to feel "royal and chosen." Show me what You have for me. In Jesus name

Who can I bless today?

What do I treasure?

1.
2.
3.
4.
5.

"they will be my own special treasure." (Mal. 3:17 NLT)

You are treasured by the heart of God. This is not a feeling, but a truth. We can either run from His love, ignore it, fight it, or let it settle down deep in our souls and fill our life. Being treasured by God can become our identity.

What does it mean to be loved and treasured by God?

"His love is "that covers my mistakes or unwise choices and whispers, "It's okay. You are forgiven and redeemed; look to Me." His love combats the voice of the accuser that tells me I should be more, do more, have more... His love settles into a deep canyon of my soul and tells me, You are worth

living and dying for. His love silences the critical voices in the mirror and says, "You are my masterpiece." (The Treasure)

God, help me to believe You treasure me. May Your love for me become my identity. Fill my heart with your love- in Jesus name

Who can I bless, help, thank, reach out to today?

What do I love about life?

1.
2.
3.
4.
5.

"If you love me, show it by doing what I've told you…" (John 14:15 MSG)

When I was a teenager, I started wondering, "Why do the right thing?" You may ask yourself the same thing.

This verse found me. Doing life God's way and making right choices is like a love message to Him. This is not about perfection or performance. This verse is about making right choices, choosing to say "no" when everyone else is saying "yes."

Do I feel alone when I make the right choice? Why or Why not?

Choosing the right thing is a way to love God. In essence, we are saying, "God, I love You more than _____ (the temptation or sin)."

If we understand God's great love for us and live immersed in His love, we can choose to show love back to Him by following His way of doing things.

God, help me to see Your way as the right way, not the boring way, and help me to choose to show I love You by obeying Your Words. In Jesus name

Who can I bless, help, thank, reach out to today?

What in my life can I thank God for?

1.
2.
3.
4.
5.

"If you love me, show it by doing what I've told you. I will talk to the Father, and he'll provide you another Friend so that you will always have someone with you. This Friend is the Spirit of Truth. The godless world can't take him in because it doesn't have eyes to see him, doesn't know what to look for. But you know him already because he has been staying with you, and will even be in you!" (John 14:15-17 MSG)

The mystery of God's Spirit living inside of us is crazy amazing! We don't have to just "try to get it right" His Spirit is always at work helping us.

What do I need God to help me with today?

This Spirit inside of us can help us in the moment where we are faced with a decision for right or wrong. His Spirt can help us with the both the big and the little things. We can choose, we are not a victim to life's temptations. He will help us. This doesn't mean that we will never sin or make a mistake, it means that we can ask for His help, and He will help us overcome.

God, may Your Spirit help me choose the right thing. And when I am tempted give me a way out. In Jesus name

Who can I bless, help, thank, reach out to today?

What are five things I love?

1.
2.
3.
4.
5.

"God is good to one and all; everything he does is suffused with grace."
(Psalms 145:9 MSG)

Do I ever feel like God has let me down? When?

Our feelings tell us, "life should be easier, that shouldn't have happened. Why is life hard? Where is God?"

Life without God *is* harder. Our souls were created with a God-shaped hole, only Jesus (His Spirit, His love) can fill. We have a choice to resist God, because life is hard and He didn't do what we asked or we can embrace Him. So many people blame God. Without realizing it we can place false blame on Him for life's stuff, people's wrong choices, humanity's choice of sin… However, God in His goodness promises to help us get through the yuck in life and give us an amazing eternity.

We get to choose what we think about God - we can let our feelings lead us or we can see who He really is by reading the Bible, looking for the great around us, asking a wise believer, and talking to Him.

What do I think about God?

God, when life is hard, I wonder where You are. If I don't feel like I measure up at times I blame You. Forgive me, I need You to fill my heart, heal my heart, and lead me. In Jesus name

Who can I bless, help, thank, reach out to today?

DAY 34

What is one area in my life that I am doing a good job? _____

Everyone wants to hear, "you are doing a great job!"

Who in my life can I tell that to today?

God gives me one word to embrace at a time. I like the simplicity of a word. One word can apply to every aspect of life. My winter word was "Trust!" I heard this word continually when I wanted to get anxious. Last summer, "Enjoy!" was my word. For me this meant: focus on enjoying the moments and not stressing about the "what ifs, unknowns, worries..." Throughout the day He reminded me to ask myself: Who can I enjoy in this moment? What about life can I embrace right now?

What would change if we all lived in one great word?

I asked a bunch of high school students to come up with a word that would motivate them throughout the school year. This word would motivate them in their walk with God and relationships with others. I was amazed by the responses: "peace, growth, diving deeper, all in, smile, learn, trust..."

What one word can you embrace for a season?

God, whisper a word to me today. May this one word change the way I think about my life. May I choose to think about Your great love for me and may Your big love spill out on others. In Jesus name

Who can I bless, help, thank, reach out to today?

What are 5 great things in my life?

1.
2.
3.
4.
5.

"Don't pick on people, jump on their failures, criticize their faults—unless, of course, you want the same treatment. Don't condemn those who are down; that hardness can boomerang. Be easy on people; you'll find life a lot easier. Give away your life; you'll find life given back, but not merely given back—given back with bonus and blessing..." (Matthew 6:38 MSG)

"Give away your life, you'll find life back."

What a crazy concept that actually works! Give encouragement, people will encourage us. Give friendship, we will have friends. Give life, and we will get life.

Who can I give life to today? How?

God, show me who can I bless, help, thank, reach out to today. In Jesus name

Who in my life is good to me? What is great in my life?

_____

_____

"_...Giving, not getting, is the way. Generosity begets generosity._" _(Matthew 6:38 MSG)_

We can continually think, "how can I give?" This thought takes the focus off our own stuff, insecurities, failures...Instead, we will look out. Doing good for others is powerful!

Who in my life needs a text of encouragement, a snap, an invitation to hang out, a compliment, or a friend?

Why not give by reaching out in some way? What holds me back?

A word of encouragement, a compliment, or a thank you is always a GOOD choice!

God, show me who in my life needs me to give to them in some way. In Jesus name Who can I bless, help, thank, reach out to today. In Jesus name

Daily, this question will be added in:

Who can I bless, help, thank, reach out to today?

What are 5 things I am thankful for?

1.
2.
3.
4.
5.

"Trust in the Lord and do good..." Psalms 37:3 (NIV)

What does trust even mean?

Trusting God involves a choice not a feeling. Have you ever done a trust fall?

Trusting takes risk. Trusting can involve an uncomfortable choice. Trusting is something that we don't always want to do. Yet if we know God is good, loving, for us - then we can trust Him.

Trusting means offering our stuff open handed to Him.

We can ask ourselves: what do I cling to with a tight grip?

What am I afraid to trust God with? Why?

Can I trust Him to give Him the thing I cling to?

Trust is a conscious choice. It brings great peace! Trusting His heart is where REAL life is found.

"It's in Christ that we find out who we are and what we are living for." *(Eph. 1:11 MSG)*

God, I choose to trust You with _____.
Please give me Your inner peace as I let go. In Jesus name

Who can I bless, help, thank, reach out to today?

What can I be thankful for today?

1.
2.
3.
4.
5.

"Dwell in the land." Psalms 37:3 (NASB)

After we trust God with our life (heart, relationships, school, work, dreams...), following His way is the best. Living the way He instructed in the Bible is not boring, it is a guarantee for the best life He has for us. He constantly forgives us when we mess up, yet continually making choices to do life His way insures the best life He has for us. "Dwell" can feel like wait. Not many of us like to wait. I like to think of "dwell" as "embrace the life God has given me."

What around us can we enjoy today?

Instead of waiting for what we are hoping for or striving for – EMBRACE today.

Embrace today: in the way we interact with people, do our work/school, play our hobby, go for our dream, treat our family, serve, embrace the life God has given us today!

What would this look like for you?

What would it look like to live every moment to the fullest?

Do you think we would enjoy life more if we embraced the life He has given us?

Let's enjoy the moments. Life is such a journey, if we wait until we get to our "destination or dream" we will miss the great things along the way.

God, remind me of all the great things around me. Help me to "embrace the life You have given me." In doing this fill my heart and thoughts with hope and peace. In Jesus name

Who can I bless, help, thank, reach out to today?

What do I enjoy? (5 things)

1.
2.
3.
4.
5.

"Enjoy serving the Lord. And he will give you what you want." (Psalms 37:4 ICB)

ENJOY! What a great word! Enjoy serving! This verse does not mean - do good and we will get what we want. This verse is talking about enjoying the life God has for us, serving Him, and blessing others around us. This may sound boring. But God knows something about our hearts, when we choose to enjoy - thinking great about life and others around us - our heart gets what it is longing for.

Enjoying and serving does something to us that is mysterious. Taking the focus off all our anxieties and unmet desires is freeing.

Instead of worrying we can do two things: **think great and invite Jesus in!**

We can think great by asking ourselves questions: "what is great in my life, who can I help today, what can I do to better myself, what can I say to someone who needs encouragement?"

We think our life into greatness. We can continually invite Jesus into our thoughts. Our current circumstances are not a determiner of how we have to feel, we can feel great by thinking great! Part of this is continually thinking "how can I enjoy others around me and how can I enjoy where I am?"

God, help me to ENJOY the life You have given me. Help me to focus on the great things and people around me. I invite Jesus into my thoughts help me to think like Him. In Jesus name

Who can I bless, help, thank, reach out to today?

DAY 40

Who in my life builds me up? What do they say about me?

_____

"Then Jesus stood up again and said to the woman, "...Then neither do I condemn you; go; and from now on sin no more." (John 8:11 NLT)

The woman Jesus was talking to was caught in a sin. People wanted to shame and condemn her. Jesus wanted to forgive her. The encounter with His forgiving love was so powerful that He told her not to sin anymore. We all sin, but I am guessing He was talking to her about the specific sin she was caught in. NO shame, no lecture, no groveling...He just said, "I don't condemn you, go...sin no more."

The voice of shame is not helpful, it makes us sit in the yuck of our sin. I have not seen shame produce change, but only lead to more wrong choices. We have a choice; listen to the voice of shame or listen to the Voice of forgiveness. The Voice of forgiveness is Jesus!

What do I feel shame about? Can I accept His forgiveness?

God, forgive me for _____. I accept Your gift of forgiveness. Silence the voice of shame. Please help me to live aware of Your voice speaking love and rescuing me. When I am tempted help me resist. In Jesus name

Who can I bless, help, thank, reach out to today?

What are 5 fun things in my life?

1.
2.
3.
4.
5.

"Live purposefully…" (Ephesians 5:15 AMPC)

Everything in life involves a choice. We get to choose to get up. We get to choose how we think. We get to choose how we speak to people. We get to choose what we do with the gifts we have. It is motivating to live with a purpose in mind!

We don't have to just think good thoughts when we read each morning - we can choose great thoughts all day.

Thinking great throughout the day will change the way we view our life, the way we treat others, how confident we are, whether we do great things.

What choices do I make every day?

Are they helping me?

Am I choosing thoughts about life that will make my life great?

God, I ask You to show me what I'm thinking that is bringing me down. Help me to choose to think great all day. Help me to be aware of what thoughts I am listening to. In Jesus name

WHO CAN I BLESS TODAY?

What one GREAT thought can I think repeatedly today?

(For example: God has great plans for me! God has unending unconditional love for me!)

What do I think when I think about God's hand in my life?

"Don't be afraid, for I am with you. Don't be discouraged, for I am your God.

I will strengthen you and help you. I will hold you up with my victorious right hand." (Is. 41:10 NLT)

What we think about God affects our life. It effects everything!!! If we think God has let us down and doesn't care, it is really hard to want to connect with Him. The enemy tells us to blame God for the bad stuff that happens.

What if God is the Rescuer from the hard life stuff? What if I am keeping at a distance or rejecting the One who will heal the sadness, brokenness, anxiety, or struggle I deal with?

What would change if I thought God wanted a great life for me?

What if I saw God as someone Who embraced me as I am and loved me in my mess?

What would change in my heart if I started thinking of God as Someone who cares for me, knows me completely, and embraces me?

Something mysterious happens when we see God as the good Father, invite Jesus into our lives, and surrender to His love and grace.

God, I am not sure I see You as You are. I invite the love and grace of Jesus to transform the way I see You, life, and me. In Jesus name

Who can I reach out to today?

What are five things great in my life?

1.
2.
3.
4.
5.

"Now that we know what we have—Jesus, this great High Priest with ready access to God—let's not let it slip through our fingers. We don't have a priest who is out of touch with our reality. He's been through weakness and testing, experienced it all—all but the sin. So, let's walk right up to him and get what he is so ready to give. Take the mercy, accept the help." (Hebrews 4:16 MSG)

When Jesus was here, He experienced the same things we do. People rejected Him. His earthly dad died. People made fun of Him. His siblings questioned Him. He suffered. He got tired. He cried. He felt His friends' pain. He came here to give us eternal life, yet maybe He did life this way so we could know that He can relate with us. He faced things we face!

Have I thought about Jesus relating with my pain, because He felt pain?

Have I thought about Jesus understanding because He lived here?

He understands, He cares, He wants to walk through the great and the hard with us.

God, I invite You to take away my pain, anxiety, sadness, and loss. Help me to invite You in every time that I feel down. In Jesus name

Who can I bless, help, thank, reach out to today?

What makes me smile?

1.
2.
3.
4.
5.

(A few things that make me smile: a warm cup of coffee, a beautiful sunset, listening to my kids laugh...)

Throughout the day, we can choose to focus on the things that make us smile.

"Therefore, let us [with privilege] approach the throne of grace [that is, the throne of God's gracious favor] with confidence and without fear, so that we may receive mercy [for our failures] and find [His amazing] grace to help in time of need [an appropriate blessing, coming just at the right moment]." (Hebrews 4:16 AMP)

The awesome exchange: we get to give God our stuff (anxiety, pain, addiction, struggle, worry, anger, sadness, failure, disappointment) and He exchanges it, giving us "mercy, grace, and blessings."

Being a person who loves pictures, I picture God's awesome throne. I picture taking Him my battle (anxiety, worry) holding it up to Him with both hands, He takes it. In exchange, He places in my hands His peace, His love, His joy. I call this the "Holy Exchange." This is not a one-time deal, it's a daily choice to give Him my stuff exchanging it for His GIFTS.

What do I want to exchange? What stuff (worry, fear, anger, disappointment, rejection, struggle) can I give God?

God, here is my _____,
please give me Your grace, mercy, peace, blessings in exchange.
In Jesus name

Who can I BLESS today?

What are five things that I am thankful for?

1.
2.
3.
4.
5.

In contrast, what do I continually stress about?

"I know the plans that I have for you, declares the Lord. They are plans for peace and not disaster, plans to give you a future filled with hope." (Jer. 29:11 GW)

If we believe that God is good and that He is for us, then we can trust His plan. We don't need to stress! Although life is not always easy following God leads to a "future filled with hope."

God is not boring! Even if God didn't promise us a "future filled with hope" following God is much better than a future filled with regret. Choices we make today affect our future. Choosing life to the fullest requires thinking great and "taking God up" on His invitation.

May we live each moment to the fullest: laugh a lot, help others, tell ourselves good things, enjoy our friendships, give our all in whatever we do, talk to God when we are lonely, live believing God is good and will give us a future "filled with hope."

What does following God look like? How can I follow God in the places He has me?

God, help me to follow You and trust that You are good and that You have a great future for me. In Jesus name

Who can I GIVE to today?

What are five little gifts in my life that make my life better?

What is one thing that I like about myself?

"The large work I've called you into but don't be overwhelmed by it. It's best to start small. Give a cool cup of water to someone who is thirsty, for instance. The smallest act of giving or receiving makes you a true apprentice. You won't lose out on a thing." (Matt. 10:42 MSG)

Yesterday God stopped me in my tracks. He said, "What little things are you doing for Me?"

That isn't what I was expecting Him to ask.

Watching the big- we can start to wonder: do the small things that I do please God?

He answered this question with a verse. A "cup of cool water"—what a small thing!!! It doesn't seem miraculous or big or life-changing! Yet God tells us, sometimes, He asks for the seemingly small. **Loving others may seem small, but it is at the center of God's heart**.

Bob Goff states, "God wants me to love the ones, I don't understand to get to know their names. To invite them to do things with me. To go and find the ones everyone has shunned and turned away." (*Everybody Always*)

Seemingly small things can look like: texting a friend, writing a note of encouragement, giving someone a ride, doing a small favor, whispering a prayer, anything!

I think God sees life so different than we do... I don't think He sees big or small, I believe He looks straight to our heart, our why, our willingness. The big is amazing and needs to be celebrated! However, seemingly small choices can help us live in constant celebration!

What seemingly small thing am I doing for God? _____. This blesses His heart.

God, when I am making a huge impact I feel good. Change my thoughts to remember You are pleased with my heart and if You lead me to small actions - they are important to You. Remind me that Jesus did the simple things like providing a meal, listening to someone's story, sharing love and truth. May I be like Him. In Jesus name

Who can I bless, help, thank, reach out to today?

What people help me?

_____

How can I thank them? (Make a list, send a text...your words are powerful!)

_____

*"He **forgives** your sins—every one." (Psalms 103:3 MSG)*

God forgives all of our sins. Knowing this can lead us to forgive others. Even if we don't feel like forgiving.

Life has taught me a few things about forgiveness:

1. Forgiveness is a choice - not a feeling.
2. **Forgetting** what someone did or said to us is *not* part of the forgiveness process. We can't always forget.
3. Forgiving is often a prayer instead of something we say or do for the person who offended us. Such as: "God, I forgive (name). I give You the hurt they caused. Heal my heart. In Jesus name"

4. Forgiveness is repetitive and it keeps our heart healthy. When we remember whatever that person said or did, we can repeat the prayer. People hurt our feelings all the time. Forgiveness leads to freedom, in contrast keeping track of wrongs leads to our own sadness and even depression.

One way to choose to have a healthy heart and forgive is to make a list of all the people who hurt us. Giving God the list of names, we can pray, "God, I choose to forgive: _____, please heal my heart and this memory. In Jesus name"

Repetitive forgiving = healthy heart

Who do I need to forgive?

God, you forgive us, so I can forgive. Yet, I need You to help me, because I don't always feel like forgiving. When I remember the hurt that person caused me; help me to forgive them again and again. Thank You that Your heart is forgiveness for all, help me to be like You. In Jesus name

Who can bless to today?

What are five things that I like about myself?

1.
2.
3.
4.
5.

If we see God as relatable this affects everything in our life!

"This resurrection life you received from God is not a timid, grave-tending life. It's adventurously expectant, greeting God with a childlike "What's next, Papa?" God's Spirit touches our spirits and confirms who we really are. We know who he is, and we know who we are: Father and children. And we know we are going to get what's coming to us—an unbelievable inheritance! We go through exactly what Christ goes through. If we go through the hard times with him, then we're certainly going to go through the good times with him!" (Romans 8:15-17 MSG)

Where do you feel like God is: (circle one)

God is a million miles away.

He is unreachable.
He is here watching, but not relatable.
He is constantly testing me.
He has let me down.
Maybe I feel close to Him (if so, what led you to this closeness).

If He were standing in front of me – would I go talk to Him or walk away?

Our feelings about God are real, yet they are not a good determiner of Who He is. He can handle our real, even if it means telling Him how we feel life (or God) has disappointed us.

God, the Creator of all, can handle our stuff. One enormous step to God is telling Him about what holds us back from a deeper relationship and commitment to Him.

In my position with God, where do I see myself?

God, I feel like You are _____.
(far away, unapproachable, close). I want to believe that You are for me, help me to see You as a loving perfect Dad. In Jesus name

Who can I bless, help, thank, reach out to today?

DAY 49

What are 5 things I am thankful for?

1.
2.
3.
4.
5.

"You are young, but don't let anyone treat you as if you are not important. Be an example to show the believers how they should live. Show them by what you say, by the way you live, by your love, by your faith, and by your pure life." (1 Tim. 4:12 ERV)

Our age is irrelevant to sharing our faith. Everyone is longing for a leader, someone to look up to, someone who is set apart from the crowd. It is easy to just want to fit in. Yet, there is more for each of us. If we embrace Jesus, people will be drawn to us, even if they do not understand our faith. If we live in God's love we won't have to broadcast our choice to do the right thing. Others will notice and be curious. People might make fun of us, but by living God's way we will be free of regret. Even though it may be hard to see at the time, we will be respected by making wise choices. Following the loving God is full of adventure.

What choices are hard to make about living out my faith?

In what ways is living out my faith an adventure?

God, help me to choose to be an example whether I feel like it or not. Help me to share who You really are by the way I live and treat others. In Jesus name

Who can I bless, help, thank, reach out to today?

DAY 50

What 5 things did God bless me with?

1.
2.
3.
4.
5.

"Guard your heart above all else, for it is the source of life." (Proverbs 4:23 CSB)

"The heart is about the size of our fist, yet holds the power of our life and death in its rhythmic consistency. Why do we ask Jesus in our heart and not our brain?" (The Treasure)

Our heart is the center of our life. We need to guard it, because it is the "source of life." If we open our heart to darkness, it effects our life and brings with it shame and guilt. If we leave bitterness in our heart, a wall grows and we become unapproachable. If we let hate fester in our heart the infection reaches every area of our life. Our heart and its condition effects our entire being!

We can ask ourselves:

How is my heart?
What hurt resides in my heart?
What hate and negativity do I resist letting go of?
Is there some darkness that I am tempted with?

Jesus came to bring hope, healing, and new life!

"This means that anyone who belongs to Christ has become a new person. The old life is gone; a new life has begun!" (2 Cor. 5:17 NLT)

Our life and our heart can be new every day in Jesus!

God, I give You my heart, shame, bitterness, pain, and unforgiveness. Please forgive me for my choice or thought that led my heart to pain. By Your great love make my heart and life new. Guard my heart from darkness, pain, temptation, bitterness, anger, selfishness. In Jesus name

Who can I bless, help, thank, reach out to today?

What are 5 great qualities in me? (Such as: I have integrity, leadership, compassion, work ethic)

1.
2.
3.
4.
5.

"Come to me, all you who are weary and burdened, and I will give you rest."

(Matthew 11:28 NIV)

Long ago, a student I was mentoring told me that she felt "heavy." She explained, "each day I wear this invisible backpack with rocks: Rejection, Pain, Disappointment, Loss from parent's divorce, Sadness... each night, I take it off before I go to sleep, but it is right beside my bed and I put it back on in the morning. Some days, I add more rocks - depending on what happens. I am just tired of carrying this." For a few weeks, we worked on unpacking her backpack of hurts. Identifying each one. Giving each one of these "rocks" to God is so powerful! Asking Him to heal the pain is freeing.

Heart healing is not always instant, yet repeatedly doing this is life-giving.

We can ask ourselves: do I wear an invisible backpack? Is it weighing me down?

What "rocks" do I fill my backpack with?

Could I unpack them and give them to God?

God, I think about this _____ (disappointment, rejection, pain) a lot. It's not helping me. Please take this heaviness and begin to heal my heart and my mind. I ask You to replace my hurt with Your love. In Jesus name

Who can I THANK today?

What am I looking forward to?

_____

Why?

_____

"For I know the plans I have for you," says the Lord. "They are plans for good and not for disaster, to give you a future and a hope." (Jer. 29:11 NLT)

God already knows the plan. He said in this verse that the plans are "good." The journey of life does not always FEEL good. However, if we choose to BELIEVE He loves us and that He is for us, we can trust His plan.

Some people fear His plan and think, "If I say, 'Yes!' to God - He will send me to the mission field." Every missionary- that I have met or read about - is so passionate and excited about their calling (with the exception of Jonah).

Our calling is what we were made for! He placed something in our heart that longs for the plan that He has in store. If we are walking with Him, where He places us is what we were created for and what our heart desires. This is amazing! He made our hearts, so He knows what is life-giving to us!

In my own life, if I am stressing about tomorrow, God reminds me by saying, "I already know the plan." Something about Him knowing brings peace to my heart. We might not know the plan, but the Creator of the Universe knows and we can choose to trust His heart for us.

Can you join me in CHOOSING to trust God with tomorrow, the future, the plans He has in store?

If not, what holds you back?

God, I want to trust that Your plans are good even when life does not always feel good. Help me to think Your truths and not to rely on feelings. Thank you for planning good things for me. In Jesus name

Who can I reach out to today?

What gifts has God given me?

1.
2.
3.
4.
5.

"You protect me with Your saving shield. You support me with Your right hand. You have stooped to make me great." (Psalms 18:35-36 NCV)

He stoops! As a child, did anyone get down on your level and look straight into your eyes?

There is something precious about looking into someone's eyes and caring for their heart. The Creator of the universe "stoops" to look into our eyes, the window of our heart.

We may wonder, "does God really care about my stuff? If you don't think He cares, why would He "stoop" down?

What does God see when He looks into my eyes (the window to my heart)?

Do I want to be seen? Why or why not?

God desires each of us. He is not just Ruler of the universe, He is someone Who adores our heart, Who is always in pursuit of us, Who longs to show us who He really is. He is pursuing you with His heart, with His love, and He is stooping to connect with you.

God, thank You for "stooping" to look into my eyes. Heal what You see in my heart, You know what makes my heart happy and sad. Help me to trust Your heart of care for me. In Jesus name

Who can I help today?

What do I like about me?

_____

What don't I like about me?

_____

Which one do I think about more?

_____

Does this affect me? How?

_____

"He knows us far better than we know ourselves... and keeps us present before God. That's why we can be so sure that every detail in our lives of love for God is worked into something good." (Romans 8:28 MSG)

Many of us believe we know exactly what we want - yet God knows our heart, mind, and soul "better" than we know ourselves. Sometimes, He gives us what we are begging for and sometimes He waits. Sometimes, He changes us in the waiting. This is not to ruin our lives, instead it is because He knows us "better."

Our thoughts about God affect what we think about Him. If we don't trust His heart for us, we might think He is boring, out-dated, slow, or just not going to come through. That is what the enemy wants: to keep us from choosing God, His plan, His way, His heart, His way of life...This is what keeps us stuck in a sin, resistant toward God, keeping God at arms-length, or just ignoring Him. This is the battle within us.

This is the battle that has been going on since the beginning: our way and what we think or God's way and what He knows.

We have a choice to choose God and His heart or choose our way.

He wants to work *every detail in our lives* "into something good." That sounds awesome. **Every detail into good!**

What thoughts about God keep me from choosing Him in every area?

Does anything keep me from trusting God in every area of my life? If so, what? Am I willing to trust His heart?

God, I want to trust in Your heart, that You will work GOOD in every area of my life. Change the misconceptions I have about You. I choose to give You me: my details, worries, insecurity, dreams, future... In Jesus name

Who can I bless today?

What are 5 things I like about my life? (Remember these when I want to think about the negative.)

1.
2.
3.
4.
5.

"But now he has reconciled you by Christ's physical body through death to present you holy in his sight, without blemish and free from accusation..." (Col. 1:22 NIV)

Once we give our lives to Christ, we are forgiven. God sees us through the lens of Jesus-perfection. So, if we already have Jesus and eternal life, why make right choices?

Our choices affect us. Great choices lead to blessings. Wrong choices lead to consequences. Some consequences for those choices show up physically, others mentally, some financially, and all wrong choices take a toll on our heart. One of the hardest things to see is a person weep over the sadness and regret their unwise choices brought.

We can ask for forgiveness and always be forgiven! Next, we can change. We do not have to stay stuck in unwise choices - we can choose to think great thoughts about our life. This often takes away the depression or desire that leads to wrong choices. We can choose to do the right thing. We can seek help if we feel stuck.

Doing the right thing takes a choice: we can choose not to gossip, not to post that, not to look at that, not to follow the crowd, not to go there, not to lie. Choosing the right thing can feel lonely or boring - yet choosing right is free from regret and consequences.

We get to choose our thoughts and actions - they don't choose us!

Inviting Jesus into our life leads to greatness! A great life is dependent on the thoughts and actions that we chose!

God, help guilt for past actions not to determine my choices today. Please forgive me for _____
. Give me strength to make the right choice in my thoughts and actions. In Jesus name

Who can I give to today?

Who in my life do I admire?

What is one quality that they have that I have also?

"A new command I give you: Love one another. As I have loved you, so you must love one another. By this everyone will know that you are my disciples, if you love one another." (John 13:33-35 NIV)

Our choices affect others! Our little choices and our big choices affect those around us. The words we say to others encourage them or tear them down. Our morale choices affect others to.

Our motivation for our choices can be: helping ourselves or helping others. Thinking great about those around us fuels our choices to help and encourage!

What choice in my life is helping or hurting someone? Is there a choice I am wrestling with that could potentially hurt someone else?

God asks us to love one another. What does "loving one another" look like in my relationships with friends, my team, my siblings, my coworkers or teachers, my parents?

Am I doing a good job loving those around me?

God, please put Your love in me so I can LOVE others today. Show me what that looks like in each relationship. I want Your love to spill out on others in my life; by the way I talk, act, think, react, and in the choices I make. In Jesus name

Who can I show love to today?

How did I live "life to the fullest" in the last two weeks?

1.
2.
3.
4.
5.

"Pray continually." (1 Thes. 5:17 NIV)

What does this verse mean?

God loves our voice. He loves to connect with us. We are never bothering Him. His heart is always tuned in to our voice. *"His ears are open to their cry." (Psalms 34:15 NASB)*

Prayer is so simple. It is a simple thought, turned into a conversation with God.

After ten years of studying prayer experts, what I realized is: talking to God is part of their day, throughout the day, they love it, they are peaceful, they like life. People who talk to God often live life to the fullest.

I want life to the fullest, don't you?

When someone pops into our mind, instead of dwelling on their life, their pain, or how they let us down we can say a quick prayer. When we are worried, we can turn our worry into a prayer. When we wake up, we can invite God into our day. One phrase, a few words, a quick thought- directed to God - inviting Him in - makes life FULL.

When we live giving things and people back to God, we live free. When we give our stuff to God, we live light, we choose happy and fun, and we can laugh.

We can start this moment. It doesn't take a routine. We can pray - while we are driving, exercising, in the shower, getting ready for school or work – anywhere, anytime. We can invite Jesus into our *every day, every moment, every relationship* by one-liner prayers whispered throughout the day.

God, I invite You into my day, my thoughts, my heart, my friendships, my struggle, my future, my life. Remind me to talk to You often. In Jesus name

Who can I help today?

What helps me "choose life to the fullest?" (Ex: laughing often, remembering something great, speaking life, trusting)

1.
2.
3.
4.
5.

"I came so they might have life, a great full life." (John 10:10 NLV)

Twenty-three years ago, at Frontier Ranch Young Life Camp, God started showing me His heart. He was so different than what I thought, for (my) God felt unreachable. I just couldn't seem to do enough for Him. Before this encounter with God, my perception of Him was not accurate.

Jesus whispered as I looked over the Colorado mountains, "I love you, not because of what you do, but because of who you are."

That day His powerful gentle whisper changed my life and this is when I began to Choose Life to the FULLEST. Why? Because His love was and is big enough to base my (our) identity on.

Living wrapped up in the unconditional love of God is life to the fullest. Everything else is a counterfeit.

These are some things I've learned about the heart of God as seen through the life of Jesus:
God is tender yet strong.
God loves each heart.
God knows every tear we cry.
God longs for relationship with us.
God adores us, quirks and all.
God forgives instead of shames.
God loves the sound of our voice.
God's love when embraced is life to the fullest!

Do you have a clear picture of God?

Do you think about His love for you? If so, does His love define you?

God, transform the way I see me, I want to see me through Your eyes of love and acceptance. I want life to the fullest. In Jesus name

Who can I bless, help, thank, reach out to today?

What do I start the day thinking? Is it great?

Ten years ago, my brother, JonMark, was playing with the Braves minor league ball at Myrtle Beach. My four kids (ages 1, 3, 5, 7) and I went to watch him play. When we got there to see him, he met us on the beach. He gave us a big hug, walked on the beach with us, and then he did something that would change the way my kids saw life. Fully dressed and in the middle of our conversation, he sprinted into the ocean, and dove in a huge wave.

Diving into the ocean, he embraces life whole heartedly. Although he faced many injuries, he lived and continues to live life to the fullest!

Multiple times, I have heard JonMark say, "I LOVE TO LIVE!

This is my interview with him about how he lives life to the fullest:

What do you think when you wake up?

"I think, "It's gonna be a great day!" Go time! Life's a party! No negativity going on, no reason not to smile, why be angry or bitter? God is good all the time!"

How do you live life to the fullest?

"Every day, is a blessing! Every day, I wake up - it's a good day - no matter what. I have a choice no matter what is going on! I woke up, so what kind of impact can I have today? WHO can I bless? I can focus on the good things like Philippians 4:8 states."

Do you have a choice? Or is thinking great a habit?

"Comes easier to some…I do think we have a choice. I don't struggle with negativity."

Do you think negative about yourself?

"No, people are so insecure about what others think, Get over it! I play for the audience of ONE, I am not defined by my abilities, I don't relate to people that struggle with insecurity, because I am not gonna get to Heaven and have God ask me about my baseball performance, it's about how we respond, how we live. God wants us to fight when it's NOT going good."

What do you do with people's negativity?

"I am a firm believer in our mind, I think: whatever you say to me, you are not gonna break me. I am going to do me, God is in charge of me.'"

How do your thoughts effect the way you see and treat others?

"It's bigger than baseball, it's life!!! How you represent yourself is very important, people pay attention to the little things, no matter what it is. Someone told me the other day, you have an incredible ability to see the best in people."

Where does God fit into life and thoughts?

*"God allows things to happen but He **will** get you through it, He is with you - fighting your fight, He wants to fight it with you, He is not abandoning you."*

What if you don't get what you want?

"You gotta accept whatever is going on in your life - no matter what. If I were in the big leagues making lots of money, I would not be the person I am today, I needed those things to happen to me to make me the person that I am."

After an injury, how did you pick yourself back up?

"Support group is key, who do you have in your life? You are who you hang out with!

"It is easier to bounce back when you are loved."

"He looks up, when He is feeling down." To read the full article search for:

July 2, 2007 North West Georgia News: *Determined - Hard work, faith help JonMark Stay Positive*

Wake up thinking great + thinking great throughout the day + inviting God into everything=Life to the Fullest!

God, I want to live my life to the fullest. Help me to live every moment as a GIFT! In Jesus name

What SMALL thing can I do today to make someone's day better?

What do I think about me? Is this life to the FULLEST?

What can I choose to think great about me? (Ex: I am kind, I am courageous, I love people, I work hard)

1.
2.
3.
4.
5.

What do you base your worth in? Does how well you do at things define you?

Our performance in sports, school, hobbies, dreams, relationships, even ministry will never fill the space in our hearts that first needs to be filled with God's love. YOU are amazing, YOU are treasured, YOU are a masterpiece! Why? simply because God made you and He loves you. If you embrace this truth every single morning, your life will be lived to the fullest, regardless of your circumstances.

This is simple, Christianity is not complex. We can let the love of God saturate our hearts (so we like ourselves). We can get to know Jesus by starting out the day inviting Him in and reading a few verses about Him. We can embrace that He loves us enough to die for us. We can let His love define us!

Why do we have worth?

What do you base your worth in?

When you think about you what makes you happy or sad with yourself?

We can replace our self-defeating thoughts by thinking, "I am special because the God of the Universe loves me, made me, and has great things planned for me."

One life-changing, truth is: "I am loved by the God that made me." (We can say this throughout the day replacing each self-defeating thought). His love gives us worth.

"And I am convinced that nothing can ever separate us from God's love. Neither death nor life, neither angels nor demons, neither our fears for today nor our worries about tomorrow—not even the powers of hell can separate us from God's love. No power in the sky above or in the earth below—indeed, nothing in all creation will ever be able to separate us from the love of God that is revealed in Christ Jesus our Lord." (Romans 8:38-39 NLT)

God, I want LIFE TO THE FULLEST! May I find my worth in Your love and acceptance. In Jesus name

What small thing can I do for someone today?

What motivates me?

"When he had finished speaking, he said to Simon, "Put out into deep water, and let down the nets for a catch."

Simon answered, "Master, we've worked hard all night and haven't caught anything. But because you say so, I will let down the nets."

When they had done so, they caught such a large number of fish that their nets began to break. So they signaled their partners in the other boat to come and help them, and they came and filled both boats so full that they began to sink.

When Simon Peter saw this, he fell at Jesus' knees and said, "Go away from me, Lord; I am a sinful man!" For he and all his companions were astonished at the catch of fish they had taken, and so were James and John, the sons of Zebedee, Simon's partners.

Then Jesus said to Simon, "Don't be afraid; from now on you will fish for people." So they pulled their boats up on shore, left everything and followed him." (Luke 5:4-11 NIV)

Reading this story over a hundred times in my lifetime, maybe five hundred, I missed something. Children ask questions, which leads me to be wowed. Reading with my eight-year old, Anden, this story led to a deeper understanding.

With eyes wide and in a very surprised voice, "Wait a minute, they left all the fish that they just caught?!" asked Anden.

His questions stopped me. Yes, I knew they left their nets and their old life behind, but I never thought about leaving the current blessing or the BIG gift that they were given. They left what they thought they longed for. Jesus gave them what they were striving for, working toward, toiling after. But after an encounter with Him, they left everything. They left the blessing, the gift, the financial gain…for Jesus.

Jesus must have been so powerful, tender, peaceful. His essence must have quenched the hunger in their souls, His love must have captured them. Which led me to think: on a daily basis, do I want Jesus and the life He has more than His gifts? To want Him the most, we must trust that His heart for us is good.

Do I long for Jesus more than what I am asking Him for?

Jesus, help me to always choose to follow You and seek You most. In Jesus name

Who can I give life to today?

What are 10 things that I am thankful for?

1.
2.
3.
4.
5.
6.
7.
8.
9.
10.

Thank you, God, for the good stuff in my life!

"...Words give life..." (Proverbs 18:21 MSG)

When we work hard to help or bless someone and we get a thank you, we feel GOOD. When we work hard and don't get that thank you - we can feel resentment. When Owin, my oldest, was six years old, his coaches (my brothers) reminded him to thank every coach after practice, every teacher after class, etc. As coaches, they realized that most people who are working with kids do not *feel* appreciated.

Looking at life from another person's perspective changes things!

Encouraging words are LIFE-GIVING! We have people that instruct, coach, manage, help us throughout each day. What if we always remembered to say, "thank you for _____(your gift, time, or encouragement)." When my teenagers notice something I have done for them and say, "thanks, Mom" I want to do more. Most people feel this way. One way to stand out and be a leader is to be appreciative!

Who can I thank today?

Encouraging words help others live life to the FULLEST!

God, thank You for _____! In Jesus name

Who can I thank and encourage today?

What do I love?

1.
2.
3.
4.
5.

When we think about what we love, we forget what we hate. We don't replay it. To live healthy, we need to be constant forgivers.

Forgiving, no matter what the offense, means we need to let it go. This includes ceasing to replay the negative words or what bothered us – and let it go – every time we remember it. Let it go again and again.

Continual forgiving works. Forgiving removes a bad feeling toward the person who did us wrong. It makes us live less stressed, because we don't spend energy thinking about the painful or negative. Forgiving frees us to think about what we love, and that is powerful.

Jesus asked us to forgive "70 times seven" - which is basically over and over and over again. He knew we would flourish as forgivers. (Matthew 18:21-22 NIV)

What do I constantly think of (that bothers me)? _____ Who do I need to forgive? _____

God, I forgive _____, because You forgive. In Jesus name

Who can I bless, help, thank, reach out to today?

What do I celebrate?

1.
2.
3.

God is whispering to each of us. Let His words of love and encouragement settle down to the deepest parts of your soul.

When I feel empty, tired, or lack of motivation, God whispers, "go to the Source." There is something mysterious about reading His Word. Most of us have heard about reading His Word since preschool. However, it is easy to resist it, or to talk ourselves out of reading it, or let it sit and collect dust. Maybe we feel overwhelmed at where to start or we feel bad for not reading, neither of these feelings are good motivators.

In contrast, when we read God's Words the Words become ALIVE, quenching something deep in our soul. Often, we find just the right word for a situation we are currently dealing with. Romans 8, John 15, and Philippians 4 - specifically in the Message translation- have been my "go to's" when I don't know what else to read or when my soul is hungry. Even though, I have read them hundreds of times, feeling the whisper of God fills my inner hunger.

His words can become the echo in our minds! The answers are ALL there, and we can jump in anytime! No "should's," no shame, just a moment with His Words can satisfy our hearts like nothing else.

"God's Word is living and powerful..." (Heb. 4:12 NLT)

God, may Your Words speak to my heart. In Jesus name

Who can I bless, help, thank, reach out to today?

What do I enjoy?

_____

"A joyful heart is good medicine..." (Proverbs 17:22 ESV)

Much of my life, my dad told me, "life is a marathon, not a sprint, ENJOY the journey."

What keeps me from enjoying the journey? _____

Among other things, worry can keep us from enjoying the journey. We worry about what others are thinking. We worry about whether we are good enough for the goal we are striving to reach. We worry wondering if we have what it takes. We worry about tomorrow.

Worry steals moments of JOY. Enjoying the journey includes inviting God into our journey, fully living each moment, and being our very best in that moment.

We live in a society where we are all striving to reach the top, but are we having any fun on the journey? So many amazing, talented people quit their dream, because stress consumes them. Exchanging JOY for worry is essential. If we choose to enjoy the journey instead of focusing on the destination; one day we will look around and realize that we are living a FULL life.

Do I enjoy each day, or I am I pushing myself so hard that my life is not fun?

God, help me to invite You into my thoughts, my words, my moments, my dreams, my journey. I choose Your joy instead of my worry. In Jesus name

Who can I give LIFE to today?

What choices am I making to live my life to the fullest?

1.
2.
3.

We are MORE!

"In all these things we are more than CONQUERORS through Him who loved us." (Rom. 8:38 NIV)

Some synonyms for conqueror are: defeat, beat, annihilate, triumph over, get the best of, overcome, crush.

People don't say, I want to grow up and be ordinary, kind of good, mediocre...No! We all long for greatness at something. Maybe we want to be great with people. Maybe we want to be great in a certain subject or field, a sport or an art. Maybe we want to be a great speaker or musician.

Our choices are a big determiner of where we end up. Where do I want to go?

What choices do I need to make to get me there?

Am I making those choices daily in my thoughts and actions?

Living life to the fullest is intentionally thinking the thoughts that will drive us and choosing to do the right thing repeatedly (even if it is boring), but there is more.

"*We are more...*" God has more for us. The secret to being more than a conqueror is not living a slogan like: "believe in yourself," or "you can do it." "*We are more than a conqueror THROUGH Him.*" If we want to do it all by ourselves, we run out of steam; we have a bad day, we fail, we feel defeated, we give in, and we have trouble overcoming things, whether it be our thoughts, our habits, our failure, our pain. By ourselves, we life defeated.

We need God to be our best. He helps us when we run out of steam, have nothing left, want to give up, and fail. He picks us up, empowers our soul, our inner drive, and uses our failure to make us stronger, so we can be more. It is our choice to invite Him in to our thoughts, our failures, our heart, our conversations, our actions, our dreams. We can choose to be a Conqueror THROUGH Him.

What do I need to conquer?

Jesus, I invite You into my failure, my negative thoughts, my best day and my worst day, my victories and my failures. Forgive me when I choose my way over Yours. Make me more than a conqueror in every area of my life. In Your name

Who can I bless, help, thank, reach out to today?

Who do I want to be? What do I want people to say about me?

In my early twenties, my mentor asked me who I wanted to be when I was 80. I wrote down a few things.

Who do you want to be when you are 80? (Will you take a moment to write down some qualities you want to live by, and what you want people to say about you?)

After asking this question, my mentor said the most profound thing, "start being that person today!"

Why wait? If you want to be more peaceful or kind. Start being that now. If you want to learn to be a prayer warrior. Start praying today. If you want to accomplish big things, start risking today.

We have today, we have this moment. We will never be able to relive this moment! This moment is a gift.

If we live like this, there is no time to waste. Why complain? Why say or post a mean comment? Why think bad about ourselves? Why miss an opportunity? Why wait to go for our dream? May we live each moment becoming the person that we want to be when we are 80.

What would change if you lived focusing on who you want to be, what legacy you want to leave behind, and what you want to be said of you?

God, I want to be _____. Show me how to become that person today. Stop me when I am wasting time being negative. I want to live each moment to the fullest. In Jesus name

Who can I BLESS today?

This makes me smile:

1.
2.
3.
4.
5.

"When we trust in Him, we're free to say whatever needs to be said, bold to go wherever we need to go. So don't let any present trouble on your behalf get you down. Be Proud!" (Eph. 3:13 MSG)

"FREE!" Don't we all want to live that way? Free from worry, free from guilt, free from that memory, free from the "shoulds" FREE! Living free makes us feel happier, lighter, more peaceful. When we are free, we enjoy life! But, how do we get there? How do we embrace the freedom God promises?

"When we TRUST in HIM we're FREE!" This sounds so easy, yet trust is continual. For instance, we worry about a goal, we can work hard on our goal, pray/give it to God, and then before we know it – we are worrying about it again. We all do this, we just don't talk about it.

Embracing God's gift of freedom requires repetition– giving God our stuff – every time we worry! We can entrust something to Him by saying, "God, I am worried about this, here is my worry, I am handing it to you, in exchange please give me Your peace, show me what to do with the "thing" that I am worried about. In Jesus name."

We might whisper a quiet prayer about a worry five times daily or 100 TIMES!

After praying, we can DO something: If we are worried about grades – we might need to study more. If we are worried about a friend – we might need to text or call them. If we are worried about the future – we might need to trust God's heart for us. We can continually give God our "present trouble" as the verse above states. Instead of holding on to our stuff, we can continually trust God with it, which will lead to a feeling of peace.

What do I need to trust God with?

God, I trust You with my life. Show me how to live out my freedom by choosing to look at the good things in my life and taking action to enjoy the gifts You have given me. In Jesus name

Who can I bless, help, thank, reach out to- today?

What are five things that I am thankful for?

1.
2.
3.
4.
5.

What do I think when I look in the mirror?

Do I think well of myself?

Would I tell any friend what I tell myself?

Early in the morning, our first thoughts about us, affect us. We carry the negative things we say to ourselves, throughout the day. Our mirror can be the place where we ruin our day. Many of us do this and don't even realize it. What if we tried something different?

What if we looked in the mirror and found something we liked about ourselves and focused on that?

What if we stopped the negativity and remembered *"we are God's masterpiece!" (Ephesians 2:10 NLT)*

If our thoughts about us changed, our feelings follow - we are happier! Our happiness will overflow and affect others, and become contagious, which will bless our relationships!

"In loving me, You (God) make me lovable." (St. Augustine)

What do I think about when I look in the mirror?

How does this thought affect me?

God, help me to see the great things You made in me. In Jesus name

Who can I bless, help, thank, reach out to today?

What makes my life full?

1.
2.
3.
4.
5.

"You are the salt of the earth. But if the salt loses its saltiness, how can it be made salty again? (Matthew 5:13 NIV)

Have you ever eaten a French fry without salt? It doesn't taste good. It's bland, and missing something! We don't want to go through life "blah" or missing out on the best.

As a Christ-follower, we get the opportunity to GIVE life to others, to be our best self, and to enjoy each day.

We get to choose how we start our day. When your alarm clock rings, what do you think?

Our first thought when we wake up can determine our day. We carry that first thought throughout the day!

If we think, "it's gonna be a GREAT day!" It probably will be. We can choose to think our day into greatness! In contrast, if we wake up dreading the day, it probably won't go well or it will take all morning to get going!

It is GOING to be a GREAT day!

Thinking great + inviting Jesus in= living FULL ➡ Affects the world around US!

God, remind me how much You love me and that You have great things for me. In Jesus name

Who can I bless, help, thank, reach out to today?

I am thankful for:

1.
2.
3.
4.
5.

"He FILLS my life with GOOD things so that I stay young and strong like an eagle." (Psalms 103:5 GNT)

Our perspective determines how we live each day. We can focus on the GOOD or the BAD - we get to choose! There will always be both.

If we focus on the good, we can see God's fingerprints everywhere. If we focus on the bad, we wonder where God is. So much of life is in the journey, the waiting, the step by step we can look around and see all the GIFTS around us. Being happy and positive is contagious and life-giving, negativity stifles and smothers the good.

When is it hard for me to think about the good?

When our brain wants to go negative, we can immediately STOP that thought and change it. We can *choose* our emotions, they don't control us.

Let's have a great day by looking around and seeing the good everywhere. When we do see the bad let's whisper a prayer, say an encouraging word, help someone. Let's not let ourselves get stuck in worry, anger, fear, resentment, or negative thoughts.

What do I think about most of the time? Do my thoughts help me?

God, You give GREAT gifts. When life feels bad help me to bring it ALL to you. You make miracles out of messes. In Jesus name

Who can I bless, help, thank, reach out to today?

What is great in my life?

1.
2.
3.
4.
5.

"But for you who welcome him, in whom he dwells—even though you still experience all the limitations of sin—you yourself experience life on God's terms. It stands to reason, doesn't it, that if the alive-and-present God who raised Jesus from the dead moves into your life, he'll do the same thing in you that he did in Jesus, bringing you alive to himself? When God lives and breathes in you (and he does, as surely as he did in Jesus), you are delivered from that dead life. With his Spirit living in you, your body will be as alive as Christ's!" (Romans 8:9-11 MSG)

"But for you who welcome Him," this phrase holds an amazing promise. As a follower of Christ, we have the promise that Jesus will never leave us. There is something beyond my comprehension that happens when we "welcome" Him into our lives, our circumstances, our thoughts, our relationships, our struggles, our worries, our challenges, our longings, and our dreams.

When we welcome someone into our home, we are excited to see them. We are inviting them into our world. Some synonyms of "welcome" are, "to receive, to meet, to embrace."

Are there parts of my life I try to keep closed to God? Why?

When we embrace, and receive Jesus daily, we are changed. We see life through His eyes. We invite His Spirit to work in us. We let go of our own stuff and "embrace" what God is doing in us. *"when God lives and breathes in you, you are delivered from dead life."* *(Romans 8:11 MSG)* We are freed from the mundane, the miserable, the status quo. We are called to something greater. When we welcome Christ into our lives, we wake up to what God wants to do in us, to us, and through us!

Jesus, I invite You in to every detail of my life, I welcome You into my circumstances, my thoughts, my relationships, my struggles, my worries, my challenges, my longings, my dreams. I give those aspects of my life to You. I embrace what You are doing in me, to me, and through me. In Jesus name

Who can I bless, help, thank, reach out to today?

What great memory can your replay in your mind? (Great memories are gifts!)

_____

_____

"See, I have tattooed your name upon my palm..." (Isaiah 49:16 TLB)

At times, we may think God has forgotten us, but our name is forever tattooed on His palm. We are special to God, even when we do not feel special. He is with us, pursuing us. He calls us by name. When He looks at us He sees straight past the fluff to who we *really* are. He sees to the core of us and loves us in that place where we feel unlovable. He loves us so much that He chose to see our name every time He looks at His hands.

How do I feel knowing God knows me, completely, and loves me fully?

God, I love that You, the Creator, love me so much that You tattooed my name on Your palm. Help me to embrace the fact that You love me whether I feel lovable or not. In Jesus name

Who can I bless, help, thank, reach out to today?

What is GREAT in my life?

1.
2.
3.
4.
5.

"For as he thinks in his heart, so is he." (Proverbs 23:7 NKJV)

If you have been reading and answering the five intro questions every morning, you are training your brain to choose great thoughts! The habit of thinking great each morning is powerful! Transforming our thoughts right before we go to sleep is also powerful!

Every night before we fall asleep, we can think about 5-10 great things in our life. We can whisper a prayer of thanks to God. I guarantee after a few weeks of doing this you will notice:

    ★You are sleeping better.
    ★You wake up well rested.
    ★You find yourself happier in the morning.

Something happens when we tell our brain that we have a great life, we start believing it, and our actions change. Something amazing happens in us when we tell ourselves great messages about who God made us to be, we start believing we are lovable, and we live out liking ourselves. Enjoying life requires thinking great about our life and ourselves in the morning and at night.

What do you normally think about before you go to sleep? Is this helpful?

God, I want to live life to the fullest, help me to think great about my life and myself. In Jesus name

Who can I bless, help, thank, reach out to today?

What are 5 things that make me smile?

1.
2.
3.
4.
5.

We think anywhere from 20,000-60,000 thoughts a day. Our individual thoughts about life, ourselves, and others bring happiness and light to our brains, or they can bring darkness.

"They did know God, but they did not honor Him as God. They were not thankful to Him and thought only of foolish things. Their foolish minds became dark." (Romans 1: 21 NLT)

This is not a fun verse! Our thoughts effect our entire mind. We can know God and still think negatively. We can repeatedly play a wrong done to us over and over in our minds. We can think about our own faults and beat ourselves up. We can think about the things we hate.

What do you think about most of the time?

There is HOPE! Changing our thoughts brings healing. We can change our mind thought by thought and eventually our mind completely changes. This is truly amazing-life-giving!

So let's be thankful instead of being disappointed.

Let's think hopeful instead of feeling drudgery, anxiety, or hopelessness.

Let's think about the things we like about others instead of the annoying things.

Let's think about how much God loves us. Then we can love ourselves and think great about ourselves.

We *can choose* to change our thoughts, which miraculously change our brain.

God, I want my mind to be full of great thoughts, cleanse my brain. I want life to the fullest! In Jesus name

Who can I bless, help, thank, reach out to today?

Am I unshakable? Why or Why not?

_____

"Jesus answered them, "Do you finally believe? In fact, you're about to make a run for it—saving your own skins and abandoning me. But I'm not abandoned. The Father is with me. I've told you all this so that trusting me, you will be unshakable and assured, deeply at peace. In this godless world, you will continue to experience difficulties. But take heart! I've conquered the world." (John 16:31-33 MSG)

In the book of John, Jesus tells the disciples that they will "abandon" Him. This is right before the account of the Garden of Gethsemane.

I wonder why Jesus told them that they would abandon Him?

I wonder if He told them they would reject Him, so they knew He was not surprised. Right after He tells them that they will abandon Him, He says, "you will be unshakable!" Only God can turn running away from Him into running toward Him.

In a way, humanity has chosen to save "our own skins." At some point, most of us have chosen our way, instead of God's way. We have chosen fear, struggle, sin. However, instead of shame or guilt, God turns our struggle into a fierce commitment to Him. He makes us strong in Him as we return, as we seek, as we realize that He is the only way. Shame and guilt keep us running. Yet, grace and love cover our mess and make us "assured, deeply at peace."

Are there ways you have "abandoned God?"

In returning and trusting Him, we will be "unshakable." May we choose Jesus. For only in Him do we find the peace and purpose that makes us UNSHAKABLE.

Jesus, Thank You that You turn messes into miracles - only You can do that. I am sorry for the ways I run from You. Please cover my sins in the blood of Jesus. I choose You, make me "unshakable" in my faith. In Jesus name

Who can I help today?

What good things has God done in my life?

1.

2.

3.

4.

5.

Thinking about the GREAT things God is doing around us and in us is LIFE GIVING! Thinking about life through a Jesus-lens takes the pressure off us. Throughout the day, WE can remember, it's not about me, it's about what God is doing. This shift in thinking takes the focus off of our performance and places our hope on God. If we live self-consumed, we forget WHO is in charge and we might miss what HE is up to. Living God-focused immediately makes us feel more secure and less insecure!!!

In his book, *Everybody Always*, Bob Goff, explains a choice we have: "It's not about me." Say it a dozen times a day. Say it a thousand times a month. Say it when you wake up and when you go to sleep. Say it again and again: "It's not about me. It's not about me." Say it when you bless a meal or do something wonderful or selfless or when you help hurting people. Make it your anthem and your prayer. We can either keep track of the good we've done or all the good God's done. Only one will really matter to us. In the end, none of us wants to find out we traded the big life Jesus talked about for a box full of worthless acknowledgements.

Which do I think about most often: myself or others?

God, may I choose today to think more about what YOU are doing and less about me. In Jesus name

Who can I bless, help, thank, reach out to today?

DAY 78

What are 5 things about me that I am thankful for?

1.
2.
3.
4.
5.

God is not playing hide-and-seek with us. He wants to be found.

"When you come looking for me, you'll find me. Yes, when you get serious about finding me and want it more than anything else, I'll make sure you won't be disappointed." (Jer. 29:13 MSG)

So much in life gets confusing. If we pray, "God show me..." HE will show us the way to go, maybe not immediately, but in His timing. *Sidenote: He never contradicts His Word (the Bible).*

If we are stuck, He doesn't want us to "figure it out" He wants us to ask Him for help. God wants to do life with us, instead of us doing stuff for Him. He wants us to invite Him in, to our thoughts, our choices, our day, our relationships, our dreams.

Regardless of how we feel, He is not distant. He is always in pursuit of us and He wants us to pursue Him back. We invite God by simply whispering, "God SHOW me...In Jesus name." This can be prayed throughout the day in any situation. When we pray, inviting HIM in, He opens our eyes to see things we wouldn't normally see.

God, show me... (what to do in this situation, relationship, choice) In Jesus name

Who can I bless, help, thank, reach out to today?

What is GREAT in my life?

1.
2.
3.
4.
5.

If I can't think of great things in my life? Maybe it is because I want to "get away" or escape?

If so, what do I want to get away from?

Maybe, the routine, responsibilities, the boring, and mundane, but that stuff is all there when I get back. So maybe it's not getting away from it ALL.

What if it's just changing my attitude about all of my life stuff?

What if I chose to like who I am and the life I have?

What if I embrace my day with excitement, my routines with excellence, my boring with a smile, and my responsibilities with an attitude of laughter?

Maybe then I would not feel like I need to get away, escape, or "veg out."

What if we approached every day every moment and gave it our best?

What would change if we are All IN - no matter what we're doing?

I think we would live life to the fullest! What if we left every conversation, every task, every practice, every day - grinning because we gave it our all? Our best attitude, our greatest effort, enjoying every moment, thinking great about others, about God, about ourselves equal no regret. If we think this way we can be "all in!"

God, when I want a "day off from life" remind me of all the GREAT things in my life. Instead of hiding or running away, help me to JUMP- ALL IN. Help me to always look for the GOOD and my this give me energy. In Jesus name

Who can I reach out to today?

What is great in my life?

1.
2.
3.
4.
5.

"...I (Jesus) came so that they can have real and eternal life, more and better life than they ever dreamed of." (Jn. 10:10 MSG)

Living life to the fullest is full of fun, adventure, hope...waking up excited to LIVE another day. Living life to the fullest is about flushing our failures and remembering great things. Living life to the fullest is about ENJOYING others around us and being at peace with the way God made us. Living life to the fullest is about GIVING our best, because we have chosen to like ourselves. We can like ourselves because God likes us. We can live FULL or we can live in FUD.

The FUD factor is always seeking to keep us from enjoying life. As a teen, my dad warned me of this. The FUD factor consists of: *fear, uncertainty, doubt.* These can creep in undetected, but they steal our zest and joy in life. We can ask ourselves questions to see if we are letting the FUD factor creep in.

Fear- what do I fear? Am I afraid of failure or my future?

Uncertainty - do I see myself as God sees me? Do I doubt my worth?

Doubt - do I doubt who I am? What God has for me? If life can be good?

If we are not loving life, others, and ourselves, there is a reason. Many times, it can be attributed to the FUD factor. For instance, thinking thoughts like: If I do this _____, will I fail? What will people think? I won't _____as good as they do. Thinking this way STEALS our happiness. These thoughts can also affect the way we see ourselves, which affects the way we treat others.

So, again we have a choice - to look at our thoughts - what we are thinking and change them. Repeatedly thinking ONE great thought can change our life! Such as: God's choice for me and love for me define my worth.

God, I give YOU my fear of _____, my doubts _____, my uncertainties about me. Please give me Your gifts of love, hope, and joy. In Jesus name

Who can I bless, help, thank, reach out to today?

What do I love about life?

1.
2.
3.
4.
5.

"Do nothing out of selfish ambition or vain conceit, but with humility consider others better than yourselves." (Phil. 2:2 NIV)

One thought can change our life! A repetitive great thought can crush all the negative thinking, change our feelings, and empower us to greatness! This truth amazes me!

Choosing one word in different seasons of life throughout the year becomes the whisper driving me. I believe choosing ONE word to focus on can motivate us to keep GOING - no matter what the circumstances. "REST, TRUST, ENJOY, RISK" are a few of my words. I encourage you to pick ONE word (or a *small* phrase) that will motivate you throughout the year.

What word (or *small* phrase) will push you when you want to quit? What word will remind you to give your best? What word will point you back to God? What word will be life-giving?

When you pick your word, you can OWN it and take it into every situation, it can be your motivating factor.

Insert your word in each blank:

What does _____ look like for me?

How can I _____ in every area of my life?

What will change if I _____?

What holds me back from _____?

God, I want LIFE TO THE FULLEST. May the word I pick drive me moment by moment reminding me to think great about life, others, myself. Remind me often of Your heart for me. In Jesus name

Who can I bless, help, thank, reach out to today?

What are five small things that make my life good?

1.
2.
3.
4.
5.

"Be kind and compassionate to one another." (Eph. 4:32 NIV)

We have more power than we realize. Our small acts can change someone's life. Saying or doing something kind can change someone's experience at school, work, on a team, etc. To us, it may not seem like a big deal; however, our kindness can be life-changing to the person we decide to bless with our gift of kindness.

Last week, I told my kids about one person whose kindness changed my high school experience. My sophomore year, I transferred to a new school with two of my best friends. But I did not have lunch with either of them. The first day, I got my lunch, and walking into the cafeteria, I realized I didn't know anyone. Feeling so awkward I walked to a table and sat by myself. Within two minutes, a girl came over to introduce herself, she had been in one of my classes. In that moment, her act of kindness in walking across the room changed my high school experience. She sat down beside me and invited me into her world of friends. Her gift of friendship was huge!

Most of us worry about how others perceive us. This worry can steal our joy and our ability to notice those in need. In contrast, when we are reaching out, giving kindness, and thinking about blessings others - we forget about our own insecurities. We enjoy life!

Who *can* I reach out to?

Who needs a friend?

What can I do to make someone else ENJOY life?

God, remind me that my life is powerful. I can influence people when I am kind. My life and words can change someone's experience. Help me to reach out. In Jesus name

Who can I bless, help, thank, reach out to today?

DAY 83

What makes my life good?

1.
2.
3.
4.
5.

Do I think about God often? Why or Why not?

"With the arrival of Jesus, the Messiah, that fateful dilemma is resolved. Those who enter into Christ's being-here-for-us no longer have to live under a continuous, low-lying black cloud. A new power is in operation. The Spirit of life in Christ, like a strong wind, has magnificently cleared the air, freeing you from a fated lifetime of brutal tyranny at the hands of sin and death." (Romans 8:1-2 MSG)

Have you ever stood still and had a huge gust of wind almost knock you over? This feels great on a hot day at the beach, the wind pushes away the heat and humidity and we can enjoy the fun around us. The "Spirit of Christ like a strong wind" is clearing away all of the things keeping us from enjoying life. The temptation, other's sin, or our own sin does NOT rule over us. His Spirit is pushing all of that yuck away. We can live FREE! The stuff that tempts us doesn't own us, the guilt that chides us has no hold on us, the inner struggle that brings death to dreams has no power. We cannot always see it, yet His Spirit is at work in us, and around us, delivering us from the "black cloud" that tries to get us down.

So how do we live free? "Those who enter into Christ's-being-here-for-us." We make a choice daily to invite Jesus in to do life with us. Daily and repeatedly, we invite Him into our junk, our memories, our struggles, our challenges, our friendships, our dreams, our thoughts, our goals...we enter life with Him. He does not walk under a "black cloud." So, when we invite Him in, the "black cloud" leaves, and is replaced with "a new power operation" - His Spirit.

The Spirit of Jesus is so *mysterious,* and it does something deep inside of us to make life amazing regardless of what we face. It is always there if we have accepted Jesus, yet continually inviting Him to do life with us gives His Spirit permission to take over and give us inner strength.

At times, do I feel a black cloud?

Jesus, please fill my life with Your Spirit. Blow away anything that gets me down. I want Your power in operation in my life. In Your name

Who can I bless, help, thank, reach out to today?

What are 5 things that I appreciate?

1.
2.
3.
4.
5.

...*"I (Jesus) have come that they may have life and have it to the FULL."* (*Jn. 10:10 NIV*)

This verse is the theme of Choose LIFE to the FULLEST! We can wrap our thoughts about Jesus around this verse. He wants a GREAT life for us, He wants a relationship with us, He wants our identity built in HIS love.

The beginning of this verse has a warning. *"The thief comes to steal, kill, and destroy..."* (*John 10:10*) I don't like that part, and yet it has a huge CLUE about how to live life to the FULL. The sneaky thief wants to ruin everything good, he is not for us. He wants to steal our joy, kill our dreams, and destroy our walk with God. He tries to taint our view of God, to make God seem boring, unreasonable, aloof, uncaring. One way the enemy tries to do this is by convincing us that it is God's fault when life hurts. The enemy steals things from us, but tries to get us to blame God. The thief is always at work to steal truth and keep us from understanding the God of the Universe, Who loves us with an everlasting, all-consuming, tender, powerful LOVE.

We can ask ourselves - is there pain that I blame God for that was brought about by other people's wrong decisions? If so, how does this affect the way I think about God?

God, I need You to protect my thoughts about life and You, show me who You are. Show me where I have misunderstood or blamed You, which led to me holding You at a distance. Heal my life and heart from things the enemy has tried to steal. In Jesus name

Who can I help today?

What are 5 things I can thank God for?

1.
2.
3.
4.
5.

What does God think when He thinks about me?

"...God has chosen you to be HIS own special treasure." (Duet 7:6 NLT)

"Throughout the Bible, God speaks refreshment to our hearts - calling us: 'beloved, My child, masterpiece, a special treasure, His friend, sons and daughters of God.'" (The Treasure)

When God thinks about us, His heart is full of love. Because God is love, it is impossible for Him to have any other reaction to us. Jesus came to show us God's kind, powerful, loving, heart for us. Jesus showed us, *"God would always love them (us) -with a Never Stopping, Never Giving Up, Unbreaking, Always and Forever Love."* (The Jesus Storybook Bible)

His love is big enough to cover up all of our insecurities and imperfections - making our heart full - so we can ENJOY Life to the Fullest.

May we sit in the truth that we are loved and adored by the Creator of the Universe as seen in the Heart and Life of Jesus.

What do I think God thinks about me?

May this question make us smile, because of His unconditional love for each of us!

God, help me to know and believe that You adore me and that when You look at me Your eyes are full of love and compassion. In Jesus name

Who can I bless, help, thank, reach out to today?

DAY 86

What do I like about me?

1.
2.
3.
4.
5.

"May my spoken words and unspoken thoughts be pleasing even to you, O Lord my Rock and my Redeemer." (Psalms 19:14 TLB)

Thinking great throughout the day is a challenge. We can start thinking about our flaws, the person that was rude, the upcoming test or project, the rejection, work...before we know it, our thoughts are depressing, so we start feeling sad or anxious, and we start acting less confident. Maybe when our thoughts spiral in negativity, we have a hard time being nice or we say things we regret. So, what can remind us to think about the GREAT, not the bad?

Throughout the day, we need reminders to remember God loves us and has great things planned for us, to look at the great things in life, to choose hope even when life is hard, to reach out instead of focusing on our stuff. If we are struggling we can ask for help.

What do you hear throughout the day that could alert you to think great? Example: school bell or set a reminder on your phone

This sound can be a "wake-up call" on our thoughts. I encourage you to find something you hear often to help you readjust your thoughts throughout the day. This practice is life-changing!

God, remind me all day, every day that You love me and You have great things for me. I don't have to think about the negative. In Jesus name

What can I say that would make someone's day better?

What are 5 great things in my life?

1.
2.
3.
4.
5.

"The Lord your God is with you, the Mighty Warrior who saves.

He will take great delight in you; in his love he will no longer rebuke you, but will rejoice over you with singing." (Zeph. 3:17 NIV)

God, the Mighty Warrior, is with us! Do we see God as a mighty warrior? Most of us love the Marvel super hero movies. The heroes seem bigger than life. We love when they defeat the enemy, crush the oppressor, and restore safety.

Do I see God as capable of doing this in my own life?

He can defeat our enemy - whatever that is. Crush the oppressor. Restore us and make us healthy. God is not wimpy. He is not absent. God is not distracted or disengaged. He is a powerful Mighty Warrior, who is with us.

A student recently told me where he thinks teens are with God, "It's not that we (teenagers) don't believe in God, we just forget about Him or don't notice Him." God is sooo powerful and big, yet we forget.

God the Mighty Warrior is ready to help us. We just need to ask, inviting Him in to our life, our stuff, our struggles, our thoughts, our day.

When we do this daily, our circumstances change and we change, which changes the world around us. When we do this, we start liking ourselves more, we feel less pressure, and we realize that we are not in control. However, we can relax knowing our loving God is in control. Our struggle might not go away instantaneously, but He will help us overcome it.

Do I see God as powerful? Why or Why not?

Do I know He is with me? What would change if I did?

God, I need You save me from_____.
In Jesus name

Who can I help today?

What do I like about my life? And Why?

1.
2.
3.
4.
5.

Focusing on the good things God placed in my life will make my day great!

"I have strength for all things in Christ Who empowers me [I am ready for anything and equal to anything through Him Who infuses inner strength into me; I am self-sufficient in Christ's sufficiency]." (Phil. 4:13 AMPC)

This verse, is used so frequently. It starts out with "I" but really it is talking about why we have strength. We have strength because Christ "empowers" us. Empower means "gives the authority or power to do something." He gives us the power to persevere, this is about Him working in us and through us.

He also infuses us with "inner strength." This means He fills us with strength. We don't have to do _____ (hard things) by ourselves.

What do I need God to empower me to do?

In what situation do I need God to fill me with strength?

God, thank You that it is not about me. Thank you that You want me to rely on You. Fill me and strengthen me through Jesus Christ. In Jesus name

Who can I thank today?

What am I thankful for?

1.
2.
3.

"Here is a simple rule of thumb for behavior: Ask yourself what you want people to do for you; then grab the initiative and do it for them! If you only love the lovable, do you expect a pat on the back? Run-of-the-mill sinners do that. If you only help those who help you, do you expect a medal? "I tell you, love your enemies. Help and give without expecting a return. You'll never—I promise—regret it. Live out this God-created identity the way our Father lives toward us, generously and graciously, even when we're at our worst. Our Father is kind; you be kind." (Luke 6:32-36 MSG)

When we love people as God asks us to *love*, we expect them to love us back. When we are kind, we expect kindness in return. Yet, God does not promise "what goes around comes around." He just asks us to love. In loving others, we give them a glimpse of His heart. Although Jesus is (and was) the essence of love. When He walked here on earth, many chose not to love Him back. This did not change His heart or His mission. He gave love to anyone who would receive it. When people respond to us unlovingly, it is usually because their heart is hurting. Their pain may be deep-rooted, they might not feel lovable. Their love tank may be on empty (I believe we each have a love tank in our heart that only God's love can fill).

When we choose to love others, the response we are given does not mean we were not loving. The response might be filtered with their own personal rejection, insecurities, and pain. We are called to love, not because others are loving us back, or because it makes us feel good, we are called to love because Jesus did.

Sometimes giving love and kindness does not feel good. We feel like the door is slammed in our face or there is no response. However, the person rejecting us might be trying to determine whether we are sincere or if we will eventually reject them. They might believe rejection is inevitable. Their response to us might not have anything to do with us, but everything to do with them.

One of my kids asked me how to be a positive influence in others' lives. I encouraged him to pick one person to be kind to everyday. Send a text. Give a compliment. Do something kind. He said, "What if the person thinks it's dumb?"

I believe, "if someone rejects your kindness, keep being kind, it does not mean that they do not like you, it probably means that they do not like themselves. All people are hungry for a kind word. So, give encouragement, regardless of the response."

Who can we give His love to today by a simple word or act of kindness?

Jesus, You give, pursue, forgive, love regardless of the response. Show me who to bless today with Your kind heart. In Your name

Who can I give life to today?

What in my life is amazing?

_____

_____

"The thief comes only to steal and kill and destroy; I have come that they may have life, and have it to the full." (John 10:10 NIV)

WOW! You finished, ninety days of thinking great and inviting Jesus in! I encourage you to look over this book and all of your thoughts.

What are you continually thankful for?

What is life-giving to you?

What helps you live life to the fullest?

Did your life feel better from thinking great every morning and throughout the day?

Your completing 90 days of thinking great created a routine in your life that you can continue always. This practice started for me when I was sixteen. Now, as an adult, I wake up every morning and write down five things I am thankful for, I whisper a thank You to God and read a few Bible verses. Then I write down a prayer or something I am worried about, and give it to God. This practice became a habit that blesses my life. Along the way, I missed a few days and that is okay. God does not get mad when we don't pray, but I find myself better, more loving, more of who I want to be when I start my day with God.

I encourage you to keep this routine. It will forever bless your life and your thoughts. God has a great life for you. The enemy will try to remind us of all the bad or the failure. But that is not God's voice, He is constantly whispering His forgiveness, His power to help us, His great love for us that knows no boundaries. May you be constantly aware that you are precious to the heart of God.

"None of this fazes us because Jesus loves us. I'm absolutely convinced that nothing—nothing living or dead, angelic or demonic, today or tomorrow, high or low, thinkable or unthinkable—absolutely nothing can get between us and God's love because of the way that Jesus our Master has embraced us. "(Romans 8:37-39 MSG)

.

LIFE TO THE FULLEST

Living a routine of Choosing Life to the Fullest might take more than 90 days.

Routines take time, if you enjoyed this book, you can go through it again or keep this routine going by:

1. Starting everyday thinking: "What 5 things am I thankful for?"
2. Whisper a prayer: "God, thank you for these things, and Jesus, I invite You into my day, my heart, my life, my words, my thoughts… In Your name"
3. Throughout the day – Identify every self-defeating thought and change it to a GREAT one. (You can do this by choosing a verse, quote, or song to replay in your mind.) This is simple, but life-changing.
4. Repeatedly think, "God is for me. He loves me, because He made me. As I embrace the love of Jesus, my life will radically change."
5. Set a reminder to do something small to bless someone every day.

NOTE FROM THE AUTHOR

"Amid my search for significance and approval, God whispered to me on a mountain in Colorado. While serving on summer staff at Frontier Ranch, a Young Life Camp, His still small voice spoke to my heart and said, "You are loved by Me. Really loved by Me - not because of what you do- but because I love you. I, Jesus, absolutely love you." (*The Treasure*) Twenty-four years ago, He whispered this message that forever changed my life.

The love of Jesus consumed my heart and continues to fill it with a love so big. This Love became my passion - to share the heart of God. My hope and prayer is that others will embrace the love of Jesus and let it transform their thoughts. It took years to undo the destructive negative thoughts that I lived immersed in. The eating disorder that I struggled with from age ten to twenty-one wreaked havoc on my identity and the way I thought God saw me. Yet, when the love of God captured my heart, my thoughts started to change. I began to "live life to the fullest."

After nineteen years of mentoring and counseling teens at The Way Counseling, I am convinced teens are continually battling their thoughts – we can think ourselves into greatness or destruction.

This book began as a short daily thoughts devotion for my own three teens. I decided to post it on @chooselifetothefullest. My kids' friends started reading. After a few weeks, I found myself teary, my own kids told me they were reading and I could see their countenance changing- they acted more positive, more hopeful, and full of joy. My seventeen-year old, who plays very competitive baseball, started laughing and letting go of the stress. My fifteen-year old daughter started giving me wise advice about what God was showing her. My thirteen-year old was grumpy with me one day said, "Mom, I just didn't start off the day thinking great." They are understanding the importance of thinking great and living inviting Jesus in. It is my hope that all who read will discover how powerful this is!

My heart's desire is to share the love of Christ through writing, mentoring, counseling, serving, speaking... I absolutely love being a mom to my five children ages eight to seventeen. My husband, Dan and I have been married nineteen years and live praying and laughing through all of the adventures that accompany life with five children.

NOTES

Goff, B. (2017). *Everybody always.* Tommy Nelson

Leaf, C. (2017). *Switch on your brain.* Baker Books

Newberry, T. (2012). *40 days to a joy-filled life.* Carol Stream, IL: Tyndale House.

Gunyon, B. (2018). *The Treasure. living immersed in His love.* Westbow: A Division of Tommy Nelson and Zondervan

Amplified Bible (AMPC). The Lockman Foundation, 1954, 1958, 1962, 1964, 1965, 1987

The Christian Standard Bible. Holman Bible Publishers. 2017

Easy To Read Version; Bible League international, 2006

God's Word. God's Word to the Nations. 1995

Good News Translation (Today's English Version, Second Edition). 1992 American Bible Society.

Holy Bible, New Living Translation, 1996, 2004, 2015 by Tyndale House Foundation. Used by permission of Tyndale House Publishers, Inc., Carol Stream, Illinois 60188.

NET Bible. Biblical Studies Press, L.L.C., 1996–2006

New Century Version. Thomas Nelson. 2005

New American Standard Bible. Copyright by The Lockman Foundation 1960, 1962, 1963, 1968, 1971, 1972, 1973, 1975, 1977, 1995

International Children's Bible. Thomas Nelson, Inc., 1986, 1988, 1999, 2015

The Holy Bible: English Standard Version. Crossway, a publishing ministry of Good News Publishers, 2016

The Holy Bible: New International Version. Biblica, Inc., 1973, 1978, 1984, 2011

Peterson, Eugene H. *The Message* Tyndale House Publishers, Inc., 1993, 2002, 201

The Bible in Worldwide English. Educational Publications, Derby DE65 6BN, UK.

Printed in the United States
By Bookmasters